BOB BARTON/DAVID BOOTH

Poetry Goes to School

From Mother Goose to Shel Silverstein

Pembroke Publishers Limited

KH

We acknowledge the financial support of the Government of Canada through
the Book Publishing Industry Development Program (BPIDP) for our publishing activities.

We acknowledge the Government of Ontario through the Ontario Media
Development Corporation's Ontario Book Initiative.

National Library of Canada Cataloguing in Publication

Barton, Robert, 1939-
   Poetry goes to school : from Mother Goose to Shel
Silverstein / Bob Barton and David Booth.

Includes bibliographical references and index.
ISBN 1-55138-161-3

   1. Poetry—Authorship—Study and teaching (Elementary) 2. Poetics—
Study and teaching (Elementary) I. Booth, David. II. Title.

LB1576.B36 2003   372.64
C2003-903410-0

Editor: Kate Revington
Cover Design: John Zehethofer
Cover Photography: Ajay Photographics
Typesetting: Jay Tee Graphics Ltd.

Printed and bound in Canada
9 8 7 6 5 4 3 2

8/16/06

Contents

Creating a Poetry Classroom

One's lucky,
Two's unlucky,
Three is health,
Four is wealth,
Five is sickness
And six is death.

Once, twice, thrice,
I give thee warning,
Please to make pancakes
A'gin tomorrow morning.

One I love, two I love,
Three I love, I say,
Four I love with all my heart,
Five I cast away;
Six he loves, seven she loves,
Eight both love.
Nine he comes, ten he
   tarries,
Eleven he courts, twelve he
   marries.

The Significance of Poetry

Having spent our teaching lives surrounded by poems and children, we are always pleased when they fit together. Poetry is a special part of childhood. It can be found in rhymes on the playground, songs in children's earphones, and students' heartfelt attempts to capture their emotions in journals. For us as teachers, poetry can be a concentrated teaching package that demonstrates language in unique patterns and forms, triggering new meanings, touching emotions, and encouraging vivid perceptions. Poems may have such a powerful impact that they are remembered forever.

About 25 years ago, Shel Silverstein gave poetry for children a rebirth and many people still read his books. While not all adults read poetry, many youngsters hold that special experience sacred throughout childhood and adolescence. Poems are, after all, emotionally condensed, meaningful moments of print that speak to children in ways that other genres of literature can't.

Poetry also provides stimulating and satisfying experiences with oral language. Children can read poems chorally—the rhythm and rhyme attracting readers of different abilities, even non-readers. The language patterns first learned by ear will later be understood in print. As they twist and turn tongues, lips, and vocal cords around unfamiliar, yet intriguing patterns, readers look closely, think carefully, and make different meanings with each reading of an engaging poem. Poems demonstrate the musicality and lyricism of our language.

Most poems demand response. Children grope towards their own private meanings and then share meanings with others. Poetry can open up histories and cultures different from their own, letting them see through different eyes and feel with different sensitivities and sensibilities.

A rich store of poetry encourages children to manipulate words and ideas in their own writing, exploring patterns of language and reworking thoughts in potent ways. It may bequeath a private and personal strength to be called on in lonely or difficult times.

Poetry also promotes play. Since words are made up of sounds, rhythms, spellings, and shapes, they can be played with—arranged, turned around, and repeated. When children play with words, they notice the sounds and rhythms of language and how words work from "the inside out." At recess and at home, children are constantly fooling with language, chanting verses, jingles, and even slogans they remember from ads. Of course, children of all ages need to observe language and all the bits and pieces that create it. As they laugh at the poems and wordplay, and puzzle over the way words fit or don't fit, children develop linguistic knowledge. As they experiment with rhyme and rhythm, riddles, tongue twisters, and metaphors and similes, they practise manipulating words and controlling the way words work. They grow as language users and in their understanding of how language functions.

How to "Eat" a Poem

The poet Eve Merriam asks, "How to Eat a Poem?" For us, there are many different ways. We enjoy reading poems aloud to children, without giving them copies, so that they can focus and fasten on to the words, the sounds of language. Through this "earprint," they may recognize and experience the power of words. Sometimes, reading poetry aloud to them feels like a ceremony—the children on the rug, or safe at their tables, participating as a community of word-lovers.

We also enjoy reading poems with the children, as a community or as a choir. Sometimes, we call out a line and the students echo it, or we take turns with every other line. Sometimes, we say a verse and the children read the next one, or we divide the class into groups for different verses or speakers within a poem. If we need to prepare copies for the children, we can write the poem on a chart or on an overhead transparency. (Better still, one or two volunteers can prepare the shared version as posters, using colored markers or individual photocopies: they can practise handwriting, careful printing, or even calligraphy.) And we mustn't leave out the computer, with its additional graphic power. A group of students may find great satisfaction in preparing copies of the poems for tomorrow's classroom poetry festival.

Having each child make a personal copy of the poems shared together can have great value. Poems kept in a poetry book or folder can be revisited throughout the year. Writing words down with care and style can have far-reaching benefits. Eddie Ing, a Grade 4 teacher, takes great pleasure in transforming, in his own handwriting, his students' poems into beautiful books they can enjoy. We value all these ways of encoding the words of our poetry lives.

If we model a great variety of poetry in our shared reading events and provide a wide selection of anthologies in our school and classroom libraries, our students may choose to read poems during independent reading times. We want to make experiencing poems in our classrooms part of a regular literacy and literature diet.

The Photobooth

A photograph is
a slice of time,
a frozen mirror that
lets you see into
your past.

That's me when I had long hair.
That's me when I learned to
  swim.
That's me with the kitten
who's now an old tomcat.

A photobooth is
a time machine.
Take a picture of yourself,
then step out into
the future.

Steve Wright

Bringing the Words to Life

We enjoy working with poems "writ large" displayed on charts or on an overhead projector, and, of course, in Big Books borrowed from the primary division. If you want to interest young people in poetry, one sure-fire way is to get them reading and performing it out loud. Chanting poetry together a few minutes a day can make an amazing difference to students' attitude towards poetry. Not only are the students enjoying themselves, they are also learning about words and their sounds. Chanting is also a way that students can learn poetry by heart without engaging in the "weekly memorizing test" approach that has curtailed the enjoyment of poetry for so many individuals.

Poems such as "For Want of a Nail" or Walter de la Mare's "Hide and Seek" possess an incantory quality which children love. But it's not just the repetition or the rhythms that appeal to them. There is something to think about, something to make them wonder. The job of poetry is to cause us to notice, to fine-tune our ears to what the words could be saying. When we encourage our students to speak poetry aloud, we are helping them to internalize the sounds of print so that when they do read silently, they can hear the words in their minds and in their imaginations.

Even words that students don't recognize often reveal their meanings when spoken aloud in the midst of familiar words. The first read-aloud of a poem might be called a "sounding" in which the students are encouraged to take risks in the way they use the words and then to become comfortable with them.

Here's how you might explore a read-aloud:

- The students can speak the words in many different ways—in a whisper, in a shout, at a slow pace.
- Try high voices and low voices.
- Sing the words.
- Speak the words with an emotional charge—sadly, boldly, timidly, or fearfully.
- Besides attending to rhyme, rhythm, and repetition, have students alter the sounds of words. Once they have given voice to the words and can speak them confidently, you can focus on details.
- Students often pause at the end of each line of poetry. Have them read for the thoughts, then insert the pauses. Ask them to consider what words should be given greater emphasis than others.
- Students can determine where voices should change from loud to soft or vice versa. What overall feeling should a voice convey? Should it sound indignant? angry? despairing? bragging? guilty? teasing? complaining? argumentative? Sharing and marking a text on the overhead projector is a good way to work with poetry in this way.

Hide and Seek

Hide and seek, says the Wind,
  in the shade of the woods;
Hide and seek, says the Moon,
  To the hazel buds;
Hide and seek, says the Cloud,
  Star unto star;
Hide and seek, says the Wave
  At the harbour bar;
Hide and seek, say I,
To myself, and step
Out of the dream of Wake
Into the dream of Sleep.

Walter de la Mare

For Want of a Nail

For want of a nail, the shoe
  was lost;
For want of the shoe, the horse
  was lost;
For want of the horse, the rider
  was lost;
For want of the rider, the battle
  was lost.
For want of the battle, the
  kingdom was lost.
And all for the want of a
  horseshoe nail.

White and grey.
High in the sky.
Interesting foliage.
Tall and thick.
Eye catching.

Old.
Absolutely beautiful
Knotty holes.

Nathan

Sally over the Water

Sally over the water
Sally over the sea,
Sally broke a milk bottle
And blamed it on me.
I told Ma,
Ma told Pa,
Sally got a scolding,
Ha, ha, ha.

What Is Under?

What is under the grass,
  Mummy,
what is under the grass?
Roots and stones and rich soil
where the loamy worms pass.

What is over the sky,
  Mummy?
what is over the sky?
Stars and planets and
  boundless space,
but never a reason why.

What is under the sea,
  Mummy,
what is under the sea?
Weird and wet and wondrous
  things,
too deep for you and me.

What is under my skin,
  Mummy,
what is under my skin?
Flesh and blood and a frame of
  bones
and your own dear self within.

Tony Mitton

Teachers can build a class repertoire of pieces that the students enjoy reading aloud again and again—rhymes, songs, wordplay—anything that brings them pleasure and fosters an emotional engagement. It isn't necessary to keep looking for new material. Many children delight in performing and hearing the same text over and over.

Every reader's voice brings a new interpretation to a poem being read aloud. The very way we breathe, the speech sounds and patterns we possess, the physical shape of our teeth, tongues, and sinus cavities, the feelings that the poem stirs in us, the attitudes of the listeners all play a part in how we speak the words and how those words sound to others.

When students read poems together, they are supported by the voices of their classmates and their teacher. As members of a speech choir, they can explore together thousands of variations to breathe life into the frozen words on the page. Students can consider these questions.

- As we read this poem, who could our voices represent?—a storyteller, an anonymous narrator, an angry crowd, a frightened family ...
- Should we establish a rhythm, or let each line determine its own pattern?
- What special words or phrases will require us to enunciate clearly?
- What mood should we establish as we share this poem?
- What feelings should we reveal as we say the poem?
- Which lines tell us to speak slowly or quickly?
- When should we speak softly or loudly?
- When should we use our high or low voices?
- Which lines should we read in unison?
- When should we use group or solo voices?
- Which lines (or words, or verse, or chorus) could be repeated?
- When could we build to a crescendo, that is, have one voice or group join in at a time until everyone is speaking? Could we do the same in reverse?
- What movement or actions could we add to enhance our reading of the poem?
- How many different ways can we interpret this poem aloud?

Dramatizing Poems

Many students need an extra incentive to enjoy the experience of choral reading—dramatizing the selection can provide this, helping them feel the music and meaning of the words. They will likely find selections that enable them to form clear images of what the words are saying most appealing. As children gain experience, they may interpret more complex selections, using sound and movement, or creating still pictures as a narrator reads the poem.

The Fruit Seller

Sumintra sits patiently
On her wooden peerha
Under the spreading neem tree
Near Mahaica big bridge
Where the river bends
And the road curves
Selling the best tropical fruits
Grown in the land—
Smooth, round, brown, juicy
  sapodillas
Short, sweet, yellow fig
  bananas
White and purple star apples
Juice running down you
  elbows me buddy
Rattling green avocados
Yellow spice mangoes
Beautiful red cashews
Insides white like candy floss
Huge watermelons sounding
Kangsing sweeter than tassa
  drumming

Sumintra awaits the arrival
Of the minibus and the
  speedboat
Waiting in anticipation
Far away from globalization

Peter Jailall

What is my country?
A place where I was born
A place strong and free
Where freedom is important
A peaceful country
Justice for all
Where everyone is welcomed
Every culture, everywhere
A proud country
My home and native land
My protector
That is my country!

Matthew

Talking About Poems

Children can talk about the illustrations, the poem itself, the poet, the content, the theme, and so on. The talk may focus on the poem's meanings, the children's identification with the poem, stories within the poem, or important background information. It may turn to the conflict, the resolution, the use of language, the difficulty of idiom, the word choice, the sentence structure, and the style. It is important that the talk return to the poem itself as a summary or reflection of the process. The children may leave the poem in order to understand it better, but they should return to see its reflection in the new learning, the new meaning that has grown from the "poem talk."

After reading the poem, the teacher can ask the students what words they liked, how the words made them feel, and how the words sounded special. These responses can be put on a chart and categorized and classified. The children can list their favorite words and phrases, the rhymes they enjoyed, the pictures they liked best, and the metaphors and comparisons they will likely remember. Children may want to draft their own questions about the poems for group work or class discussion. They can jot down their thoughts and feelings as they are reading each poem, perhaps on a stick-it note, almost in a stream of consciousness. Doing this may help them to understand their own processes of reading poetry and contribute to the discussion after the poems have been read.

Writing Poetry

A poem allows us to say things in a special way. Since playground verse usually rhymes, many children are convinced that poetry must always rhyme. Hearing lots of poems read aloud will help children appreciate the variety of forms open to them and "mentor" their writing efforts.

Manipulating chants and cheers by substituting words and lines is an easy way to begin working with poetry. Imposing a slightly unusual pattern, such as that of an acrostic, in which the initial letters of each line form a word or phrase, can help distract the children from the artificial constraints of rhythm and rhyme. Some, however, will see free verse as an effective means of expression from the beginning.

Teachers can help children sense the aesthetic power of a poem, highlighting a special word, a particular image created, or a pleasing juxtaposition of words. When children begin to notice the affective side of poetic language, they are coming to understand the nature of poetry.

How to Support Poem Makers

If we want children to truly become poem makers, we need to create a classroom where they feel safe in revealing their deepest feelings. We can't expect children to express what really matters unless they know for certain that their words will be respected and their thoughts secure; achieving this may require that some writings remain private, tucked inside their notebooks, or shared with just the teacher. Often, we can help them to select a portion that can be reworked or restructured for sharing, as all effective editors would do in the world of publishing. Georgia Heard says that words from the heart are entrusted gifts. Emotional responses can't be demanded; they must be nurtured.

- Children's notebooks are magic resources for poem making. The details and events of their everyday lives, caught in the moment like Polaroid pictures, provide the raw data for later use in poem making. Children can take from those captured moments—the sights and sounds and memories conjured up—and transform one or two into a poem. The bits and pieces in their notebooks can awaken their imaginations.
- Children can write poems drawn from school incidents, their life memories, their observations of objects or places that matter to them, their own problems, their world concerns, the wonders that generate even more questions (what Ralph Fletcher calls "fierce wonderings" and "bottomless questions"), the stories that touch them, and other poems that intrigue them. Often, the book that a child is reading will offer occasions for poem making: something a character does or says or doesn't say; a plot event that reeks of unfairness to a young poet; a memory triggered by the text; a need to continue writing down the future life pathway of a character.
- Some children fill their notebooks with drawings and sketches as well as words. These tentative images can be developed into word pictures, observations in print and shape that morph into poems. Ideas come in all kinds of packages, and words and pictures often say more together than they can alone. Watercolors, prints, colored markers, colored printers, photocopied collages—all fill the aesthetic need in children.
- Mentor poems generate powerful support for children new to poetry making. By highlighting particular poems and poets in read-aloud time or in a mini-lesson, teachers can reveal patterns and shapes and structures and ideas for children to borrow or tap into in designing their own creations. Often, a young writer will stick closely to the mentor poem, but as the writing develops, suddenly the work takes wing and the young poem maker twists and turns his own lines into a personal creation. The shadow of the original now filters through the new interpretation, and the child stands on the shoulders of his mentor.
- Fill your classroom with examples of "words that taste good." They will come from things the children say, often accidentally, from the stories they are reading, from "found" poems someone discovers inside a textbook or a notice, from games or current events. You and the children can record these words and expressions on a word wall, on a bulletin board or chart, or even on a class Web site. Think of these surprise finds as "poetic graffiti," and take delight in the power and wonder of everyday poem moments. Then children will become word finders themselves.
- Teachers can celebrate the unique way that individual children make sense of their world and encourage the sharing of their poems as demonstrations of who they are and how they represent their views and perceptions. Like our handwriting, our poems reveal characteristics that only we possess. Poem makers can begin to find visions of self as they compose inside their own skins.

- We can try to think of poems as normal responses to a variety of stimuli in our teaching program, and not just as a once-a-year unit. They can be included in a science centre, seen as integral to a social studies topic, and featured as important voices in a novel study. We need to have them in letters to parents, as end-of-year student booklets, as responses to student dialogue journals, as songs, as interconnections to art projects, and as thank you's for guest speakers.

- A poetry-enriched classroom will be full of mentor poetry books, laminated posters of children's poems, bulletin boards of art reproductions, artifacts from nature that promote close observation and inspiration, tapes of poets and children and teachers reading poems, and personal folders for each child of favorite poems read or written.

- Children need to experience a wide variety of genres, styles, shapes, and ideas in their poems: silly rhymes, funny stories, complicated patterns, different voices, complex themes, harrowing issues, different viewpoints, intense feelings, and personal connections as well as other cultures. School is the main hope for children to meet the world inside a poem. We need to search for poems that are significant to us and the children. Community property.

- Poem makers need access to all kinds of paper and utensils for writing. Great rolls of mural paper allow poems to be suspended from the ceiling. Beautiful sheets of paper demand careful revision before the final outcome. Multicolors of markers and paints and inks celebrate the special needs that some words require.

- We can engage poem makers in the craft of poetry, as they explore how poems and poets work by reading and writing poetic language. Children need opportunities to recognize and employ the tools that poets use: the sounds of poetry (rhythm, rhyme, repetition, alliteration, onomatopoeia, stress, pauses); the techniques (metaphor, simile, personification, voice, tense, strong verbs, a provocative title); and the patterns of poems (fragments of poetic language, free verse, lists, haiku, ballad, limerick). Repetition, refrains, and echoes often add rhythm and style to a child's writing. Like ice skating, where drills are better practised while wearing skates, the craft of poetry is internalized through reading and writing poems that matter to the children. Children need to understand that poetic language has its own qualities and appearances; it looks and behaves differently from much of prose.

- Young poem makers need to feel the playfulness of working with words and ideas inside poetry forms. They need to write quickly and try to capture all of their thoughts, to cross out words and rearrange lines, sometimes laughing out loud at their own cleverness. They need, as Donald Graves says, to keep their work open-ended, to welcome new ideas and different ways of encoding them. The brain and the imagination work faster than the hand or keyboard, and poems are always in transformation. Revisiting a poem later can offer new energy for rewriting.

- Revision is a useful means of building poetry strength. Finding ways to motivate poem makers into wanting to revisit and rework their poems takes teaching skill, but it helps to have procedures and strategies built into your program: children need lots of editing-free games and exercises with wordplay and wordcraft, alongside their times for intensive poetry writing; they need to know the support and assistance that conferences with the teacher can offer; they require management techniques for scheduling times and places for revising; they need folders for their different drafts, as well as computer access and references; they need to build some pieces they have written into major writing events, and to keep others as works in progress, or as ideas that might be developed later; they need times for sharing their work, and opportunity for reflection; they need to publish some of their poems in a variety of modes and mediums. They need to know that they are revising their writing to add power to their poems.

How Computers Can Enhance Poetry Writing

Olivia O'Sullivan and Claire Warner, with the Centre for Literacy in Primary Education, created a helpful outline for incorporating computers and informational technology into programs to support poetry writing. Here is a summary of what students can do:

Teachers find that on-screen activities promote children's purposeful talk. The screen offers a public focus for a group of children working together. To promote talk, it is best that children work in twos or threes.

- They can compose and change texts with ease, for example, using the Do and Undo buttons in a word-processing program or cutting and pasting a section of text in order to change the structure of a piece of writing.
- They can play with language—"virtual" play with words on screen is similar to learning through physical play.
- They can integrate a range of different media into a single text—sound, images, and animations—with a range of fonts, styles, headings, and formats.
- They can publish and share texts electronically, something that enhances well-established notions of communication, audience, and purpose as a powerful motivational force for writing.

Reordering parts of a poem helps children to focus on the poem's meaning and structure. This approach involves use of the highlighter pen facility in Microsoft Word. You can use the highlighter pen to select particular phrases or images from a piece of descriptive prose. Children can then delete unwanted words and are left with the most powerful parts of their writing to develop into a poem.

- They can use word processing with a poem or group of poems to draw attention to either whole text or within-text features (e.g., rhyme, particular kinds of language, and patterns).
- Students can highlight, drag and drop, or cut and paste to sort the verses of a poem such as a ballad into the order they find most meaningful.
- Students can create Web pages.
- Student poets can get their work published on school Web sites or turn to on-line Web authoring facilities to create Web sites.
- Students can use the Internet to gain almost instant access to a wealth of information about poets and poetry. Useful sites include these:
  http://bbc.co.uk/arts/poetry/index.shtml
  www.poetryzone.ndirect.co.uk/guest.htm
  http://panmacmillan.com/CB/poetry
  http://www.puffin.co.uk
  http://www.mystworld.com/youngwriter
  http://www.poetrysoc.com.education
  http://bbc.co.uk/education/listenandwrite
  http://rhymezone.com

www.schools.uk.com provides a facility to create your own school or class Web site. The larger Internet service providers also usually provide free Web space for a Web site, if you sign up for an account with them. For example, you can create a free Web site using Freeserve once you sign up at www.freeserve.co.uk.

- Students can also check out Poets Corner, at www.poets-corner.org, a user-friendly public library of poetic works which also offers suggestions for further reading and a growing index of published books of poems, listed by author.
- They can e-mail poets, such as Jon Hegley, the BBC resident on-line poet, with questions and comments.

Choosing Poems to Share

We are always on the lookout for new poetry anthologies, and our friends and colleagues support us in this quest. We find Web sites becoming more helpful, and we always check the poetry shelf when we visit a bookstore or library. In general, we like poems that tell a story or possess a rich sound quality. We also look for pieces with short lines that are easy on the eye, memorable to the ear, and well paced for speaking.

Reading three or four poetry anthologies in an evening is a pleasure for us, a chance to revisit the words and rhythms of childhood and to hone our ability to select those few poems that we hope will reach a given group of young people. Our collection of poems grows and grows.

Collections of traditional verse are a good place for you to begin looking. Poets such as Charles Causley, Dennis Lee, Michael Rosen, Jack Prelutsky, Sheree Fitch, Eve Merriam, Robert Priest, and Grace Nichols have much to offer. Encourage students to browse through poetry anthologies to find pieces they would like to read aloud and add to the class collection. Many contemporary pieces are musically inspired and take their cue from rap, reggae, rock, funk, and jazz. Students can tape-record one another's selections and experiment with ways of bringing alive their choices.

At the end of each of the book's eight chapters, you will find brief poet biographies and listings of key poetry books. Be sure to investigate these poets further and to use some of the recommended resources in your classroom. Let your students hear, read, and enjoy a variety of vibrant poetic voices.

Celebrating Poets

We want to help children see poets as working artists, part of our language and literacy community. One way to foster this sense of connection with poets is by having guest poets in the classroom. Sometimes, they are sponsored by government agencies or school councils. Sometimes, they are local poets happy to have an audience for their work.

We can also direct students to books of interviews with poets for young people, as well as dozens of Web sites featuring information about poets' lives and interests. Check out some of the Web sites noted under "How Computers Can Enhance Poetry Writing."

You can use the profiles provided at the end of each chapter to prompt poet studies. Students can start with the brief biographies, as well as the poetry book lists, and organize poet celebrations. They can present readings, prepare posters, write expanded biographies, gather as much of a poet's work as possible, and share other information downloaded from Web sites. By recognizing poets in such ways and having their poems filling the classroom, we honor them and their work as wordsmiths.

Sea Timeless Song

Hurricane come
and hurricane go
but sea—sea timeless
sea timeless
sea timeless
sea timeless
sea timeless

Hibiscus bloom
then dry wither so
but sea—sea timeless
sea timeless
sea timeless
sea timeless
sea timeless

Tourist come
And tourist go
But sea—sea timeless
sea timeless
sea timeless
sea timeless
sea timeless

Grace Nichols

"We all need someone to point out that the emperor is wearing no clothes. That's the poet's job."—*Arnold Adoff*

What Students Are Doing in a Poetry Classroom

❏ Listening to poetry read aloud by the teacher, peers, guest poets, and older students on tapes, CDs, and video

❏ Interpreting poems collaboratively with a partner, in groups, as a class

❏ Learning the history of poetry, beginning with Mother Goose and other examples from the oral tradition

❏ Learning about the history of language through poetry

❏ Exploring the oral nature of poetry through colloquial verses, skipping rhymes, ballads, jokes, street rhymes, and advertising

❏ Reading poems from other cultures, other places, and other times, including poems in different dialects and languages, and poems from Canada, the United States, England, and the Caribbean

❏ Building their own collections of anthologies of poems both read and written

❏ Browsing through single poet collections and various types of anthologies

❏ Conducting surveys of poetry tastes and attitudes

❏ Reading and appreciating both classic and contemporary poets

❏ Comparing, classifying, and categorizing poems by themes, poets, and styles

❏ Reading poems aloud informally, in groups, and with partners or reading buddies

❏ Discovering a variety of patterns in the poetry they have heard and read

❏ Recognizing and understanding different types of rhythm and rhyme, including free verse

❏ Noting repetitive sequences, refrains, and choruses in poems

❏ Recognizing and using alphabet and number patterns as poetry

❏ Becoming aware of cultural patterns and sequences in poems

❏ Reading and writing poems using different formats: haiku, limerick, riddle, tongue twister, acrostic, rhyming couplets, free verse, and so on

❏ Finding the stories inside and outside the poems

❏ Recognizing and using parody and satire in poems

❏ Noticing the relationship of visual arts and poems in picture books and anthologies

❏ Exploring poems through conversations

❏ Discussing their ideas generated by the poem

❏ Exploring games, rituals, and ceremonies in poetic forms

❏ Solving and adding to cloze procedures in rhymes

❑ Exploring sounds and songs through poetry

❑ Sharing and performing poems aloud, with movement and music and sound

❑ Interpreting poems through Readers Theatre

❑ Recognizing monologues and dialogues in poetry

❑ Improvising and role-playing from poems

❑ Becoming aware of poetic writing in scripts, novels, and information texts

❑ Noting points of view inside poems

❑ Noting and using metaphors, similes, analogy, onomatopoeia, and personification in poems

❑ Noting the use of connotation and denotation of special words

❑ Writing poems drawn from observations and memories of personal experiences recorded in notebooks

❑ Innovating on predictable patterns in poems and creating their own versions

❑ Integrating the arts alongside their poetry, illustrating and drawing alongside their poems

❑ Painting word pictures and portraits with the words of their poems

❑ Writing information, research, instructions, and opinions in poetic forms

❑ Noting and incorporating new and different words in their poetic writing

❑ Recording and later incorporating special words and phrases in their writing of poems

❑ Observing and recording found poems in the environment

❑ Transforming from one mode to another (e.g., from prose to poetry)

❑ Formatting, revising, and editing using the computer

❑ Finding suitable formats and shapes, using calligraphy and art, for composing poems

❑ Memorizing favorite poems from their poetry folders

❑ Recognizing and understanding that poetry's sounds are not just limited to the literal noises that words make but include the voice (teasing, guilty, complaining)

❑ Recognizing interpretation and appreciation as a cumulative and continuing process of discovery

CHAPTER 1

The Patterns in Poems

If All the Seas Were One Sea

If all the seas were one sea
What a great sea that would be.
If all the trees were one tree
What a great tree that would be.
If all beings were one being
What a great being that would be.
If all the axes were one axe
What a great axe that would be.
And if the great being took the great axe
and chopped down the great tree,
And if the great tree fell into the great sea
What a great SPLASH that would be.

This Is the Key of the Kingdom

This is the key of the kingdom
In that kingdom is a city,
In that city is a town,
In that town there is a street,
In that street there winds a
 lane,
In that lane there is a yard,
In that yard there is a house,
In that house there waits a
 room,
In that room there is a bed,
On that bed there is a basket,
A basket of flowers.

Flowers in the basket,
Flowers on the bed,
Bed in the chamber,
Chamber in the house,
House in the weedy yard,
Yard in the winding lane,
Lane in the broad street,
Street in the high town,
Town in the city,
City in the kingdom:
This is the key of the kingdom.

Poems with predictable patterns provide a useful entry point in bringing poetry and children together. Patterns inside poetry can help children to read texts that are more challenging than they realize. Success with patterned poems can contribute to the children's knowledge of words, language conventions, and poem structures. Teachers can draw their attention to aspects of each of these topics (e.g., new words, the function of punctuation in a line, structures particular to a kind of poem). When children meet poems filled with rhymes and rhythms, rich in repetitions and refrains, they may join in spontaneously.

Children may innovate on a poem pattern they have enjoyed. When they do so, they use their knowledge of the underlying structures in order to compose their own poems. Children borrow their favorite literary structures, expanding their linguistic storehouse, transforming and reshaping the borrowed language, and tuning their ears to the power of the poem.

This chapter explores many types of poem patterns—rhymes, rhythms, shapes, forms, and styles—all of them "hangers for words," ways of arranging our ideas and feelings so that we see them anew.

Rhyming Our Way into Poetry

The Quarrel

I quarreled with my brother,
I don't know what about,
One thing led to another
And somehow we fell out.
The start of it was slight,
The end of it was strong,
He said he was right,
I knew he was wrong!

We hated one another.
The afternoon turned black.
Then suddenly my brother
Thumped me on the back,
And said, "Oh, come along!
We can't go on all night—
I was in the wrong."
So he was in the right.

Eleanor Farjeon

Before the printing press, bards wove rhyme and patterns into their stories to make them memorable. Popular songs, most rap songs, and many poems continue this trend today. Nursery rhymes, intended for the ear, have been repeated for centuries. Many poets use sophisticated rhyming schemes to effect emotional twists and surprises in their writings.

Today's poets for children often save rhyme for humorous themes or for rhythmic verse. We enjoy reading rhyming poems chorally as the whole class joins in, following the invisible bouncing ball as the rhythm drives us forward.

Many teachers discourage their students from writing rhymed poems, however. English vocabulary has relatively few words that rhyme and for beginning writers, using rhymed words in poems too often leads to the clichéd and banal banging of words, like "fight" and "might," or "love" and "dove." A few words in English are thought to have no perfect rhyme: orange, sugar, radio and elephant.

It is helpful for children to notice how rhyme works through reading and hearing different selections with different types of rhyme. They might note the repetition of a sound falling at the end of a line, rhymes buried within a poem, or the occasional rhyme used sparingly to give power to a poem.

- Children can write short two-line nonsense verses for a class book. They can brainstorm a list of unrelated rhyming words, pairing unusual, humorous words. Perhaps they could use the names of characters from TV shows as a basis for their rhymes. They may want to explore rhyming dictionaries in composing their own poems.
- Using different anthologies, children can search for unusual rhymes, words that rhyme in different ways ("the blowing wind, the busy mind"), rhymes inside lines, rhymes that don't seem to work, the rhyming words with the most syllables, and poems that use the same rhyme scheme, for example, *a b a b*.

Rhyme Control

Much of today's modern verse doesn't use rhyme in the same ways as traditional poetry. Playing and experimenting with words and sounds is good exercise for the imagination and can strengthen your word power.

- Some rhymes are exact, some inexact, and some kept apart. Can you find examples of these in "The Mirror"?

The Mirror

Mirror mirror tell me
Am I pretty or plain?
Or am I downright ugly,
And ugly to remain?
Shall I many a gentleman?
Shall I marry a clown?
Or shall I marry
Old Knives and Scissors
Shouting through the town?

Robert Graves

- Take the first two lines of the Michael Rosen poem that follows and invent two new lines of your own to finish it.

Down behind the dustbin
I met a dog called Sid.
He said he didn't know me,
but I'm pretty sure he did.

Here's an example of what Michael Rosen did:

Down behind the dustbin
I met a dog called Sid.
He could smell a bone inside
but couldn't lift the lid.

- Change the name of the dog and add new lines.

- Write your own rhyming piece using the format of this traditional rhyme which repeats the same word four times.

Papa Moses killed a skunk
Mama Moses cooked the skunk
Baby Moses ate the skunk
My oh my how they stunk!

Rhyming Time

The Hen

The hen is a ferocious fowl,
She pecks you till she makes you _____ .

And all the time she flaps her wings,
And says the most insulting _____.

And when you try to take her eggs,
She bites large pieces from your _____.

The only safe way to get these,
Is to creep on your hands and _____.

In the meanwhile a friend must hide,
And jump out on the other _____.

And then you snatch the eggs and run
While she pursues the other _____.

The difficulty is, to find
A trusty friend who will not _____.

- Fill in the blanks of the poem above. How many different rhyming words can you discover for each blank? You might use a rhyming dictionary.
- Make a class list of all the suggestions. Are there any words with more than one syllable?
- You can work in small groups for this next activity. First, select one or two poetry anthologies. Then, find a poem with an obvious or heavy rhyme.
- Now, work in your groups to prepare a "game poem." Using "The Hen" as a model, omit various rhyme words.
- Present your "game poem" aloud or on an overhead projector transparency. Let your classmates fill in the blanks.
- Which were the most unusual words that your classmates found?
- *Class Puzzle:* Can you find rhymes for these words? (It may take two words to make a rhyme.)

hippopotami   television   poetry   thunder   tangerine

Feeling the Rhythm

The word "rhythm" comes from the Greek. It means measured motion. Rhythm in poetry is like the beat in music. Reading and writing poems offers you opportunities to experiment with a variety of rhythms. In many poems, we clap our hands or move our feet because rhythm is best learned through the body, not just through the brain.

Biking

Fingers grip,
toes curl;
head down,
wheels whirl.

Hair streams,
fields race;
ears sting,
winds chase.

Breathe deep,
troubles gone;
just feel
windsong.

Judith Nicholls

- The poem "Biking" has a strong rhythmic pattern. Try to say the poem in one breath, or stop at the end of each verse.
- Break into three groups. Try the poem as a round, each group beginning after the previous group reads the first line.
- Try writing a group poem about skateboarding, rollerblading, or surfing. How will you determine the rhythm? Will you want two or three words a line? How will you create tension? See how the poem below reflects the pattern of rain.

The Rain

The rain is raining all around,
It falls on field and tree;
It rains on the umbrellas here
And on the ships at sea.

R. L. Stevenson

All in Together

Rhyme, rhythm, and repetition make "Natasha Green" ideal for chanting.

Natasha Green

Natasha Green
Natasha Green
Stuck her head
in a washing machine

Washing machine
Washing machine
Round and round
Natasha Green

Natasha Green
Natasha Green
Cleanest girl
I've ever seen

Ever seen
Ever seen
A girl with her head
in a washing machine?

Washing machine
Washing machine
Last home of
Natasha Green

Natasha Green
Natasha Green
washed away
In a white machine

White machine
White machine
Soaped to death
Natasha Green

Natasha Green
Natasha Green
cleanest ghost
I've ever seen

MORAL
Washing machines are for
Knickers and blouses
Washing machines are for
Jumpers and trousers
Keep your head out of
The washing machine
Or you'll end up as spotless as
Little Miss Green.

Ian McMillan

Try some of the following ideas.

- Read the poem out loud in unison.
- Divide the poem into solos and choruses and read it again.
- Add a body beat with the words. For example, you could snap your fingers, then clap your hands.
- Experiment with ways to incorporate sound effects. (For example, some students could chant "Wash, wash" as the other students read the lines.)
- Divide into eight groups. Each group takes a different verse and invents a movement pattern to accompany their lines.
- Share all the verses of the poem, movements included. Everyone can read the final verse.

A Two-Part Round

Puss came dancing out of the barn
With a pair of bagpipes under her arm;
She could sing nothing but Fiddle cum, fee
The mouse has married the bumble bee
Pipe cat, dance mouse,
We'll have a wedding at our good house.

This rhyme is found in a variety of forms. The earliest recorded version appears to be that in a Wiltshire manuscript dated 1740:

Fiddle-de-dee, fiddle-de-dee!
The wasp has married the bumble bee!
Puss came dancing out of the barn
With a pair of bagpipes under her arm.
One for Johnnie and one for me,
Fiddle-de-dee, fiddle-de-dee!

Here is another version:

Fiddle-de-dee, fiddle-de-dee,
The fly shall marry the bumble-bee.
They went to the church, and married was she:
The fly has married the bumble-bee.

- Reread the first version of the poem. It has wonderful toe-tapping rhythms.
- Try speaking the poem as a two-part round. Half the class can begin and the other join in after "under her arm." Both groups can say the piece twice.
- Do the piece again, but add stomping and clapping on the line "Pipe cat, dance mouse."
- Can your group create an old-fashioned dance with advancing and retreating lines? End the dance with the players forming a funnel. Who will say the words aloud as the dancers move?

Freeing the Verse

Free verse describes lines of poetry written without regular beat and rhyme. One of the first great poets to use the form was the American Walt Whitman.

Free verse does not ignore the traditional rules of poetry, but the poets who write in this form follow their own set of rules, based on personal thoughts and feelings, the patterns of speech, and a sense of how the poem should look on the page. Each free verse poem must be a true poem, not a careless jumble of words. Poets find their own heartbeats, rather than following pre-set patterns. The lines in the poems are determined by the flow of ideas rather than by the count of syllables.

Grandpa

Grandpa's hands are as rough as
    garden sacks
And as warm as pockets.
His skin is crushed paper round
    his eyes
Wrapping up their secrets.

Berlie Doherty

- You can explore free verse with the class by reading several poems in this style. "Grandpa," above, is one example. The students can notice how the ideas and feelings are represented on the page, and discuss what makes them poetry and not prose. Do they think there is "poetic prose"?
- Select a paragraph from a novel that students have been reading and write it on a transparency. The students can explore poetic form by breaking the lines at different places and comparing effects.
- Invite the students to choose a poem they like and break it up into a variety of different lines. If they have access to a computer, they can try different fonts and sizes of words and letters, and make several versions of the poem: one with long lines, one with short lines, or one word per line, until a meaningful shape for the poem begins to emerge. They may want to add words or descriptions, or eliminate some. The placement of just one word can alter a whole poem. One student created a new version of "Grandpa."

Grandpa's hands
Are as rough as
Garden sacks (and as warm as pockets).
His skin is
Crushed paper
Around his eyes (wrapping up their secrets).

> Whatever kind of poem it is, the language usually has a pattern. Rhyming is one way of patterning words. Free verse uses all kinds of other patterns, as well as an occasional rhyme.

Using Everyday Patterns

The Trusty Old Alphabet: A Demonstration

A was an archer, who shot at a frog,
B was a butcher, and had a great dog,
C was a captain, all covered with lace,
D was a drunkard, and had a red face.
E was an esquire, with pride on his brow,
F was a farmer, and followed the plough,
G was a gamester, who had but ill-luck,
H was a hunter, and hunted a duck,
I was an innkeeper, who loved to carouse,
J was a joiner, and built up a house.
K was King William, once governed this land,
L was a lady, who had a white hand.
M was a miser, and hoarded up gold,
N was a nobleman, gallant and bold.
O was an oyster girl, and went about town,
P was a parson, and wore a black gown.
Q was a queen, and wore a silk slip,
R was a robber, and wanted a whip.
S was a sailor, and spent all he got,
T was a tinker, and mended a pot.
U was a usurer, a miserable elf,
V was a vintner, who drank all himself.
W was a watchman, and guarded the door,
X was expensive, and so became poor.
Y was a youth, that did not love school,
Z was a zany, a poor harmless fool.

In America, the above rhyme was printed in Boston as early as 1761. In the first half of the nineteenth century, several alphabets began "A was an archer." There was a couplet for each letter:

A was an archer and shot at a frog,
But missing his mark shot into a bog.

The class can go on an "alphabet search" for picture books structured around the alphabet. As they read them, they can share the ones that incorporate different rhyme schemes.

The students in Jo Phenix's class brainstormed to find rhymes for each letter and create a pattern book based on the nursery rhyme "A Was an Apple Pie." The brainstorming of the story line was done as a group, and individual children then chose pages to illustrate.

A was an airplane.
B built it.
C cleaned it.
D dusted it.
E entered it.
F flew it.
G gassed it up.
H heard it take off.
I iced up the wings.
J just landed it.
K kept the key.
L looped the loop.
M made the engine.

N named it.
O opened the door.
P piloted it.
Q quit the job.
R rode in it.
S stopped it.
T towed it.
U unfastened the seat-belt.
V vacuumed it.
W watched the movie.
X exited.
Y yawned on it.
Z zoomed into the air.

Your class can create their own alphabet poems in a similar fashion.

- It may be more effective to have students work in partners or small groups; you can provide a theme, such as transportation or fast food, to start them off.
- Children can do a lot of research creating ABC books in the classroom. For example, they don't know many words beginning with *Q*, and they may find it interesting to make a list and decide which one they can use in their story. They can then look for words they can use for *X* and other more difficult letters. Here, they were starting from a book called *Q Is for Duck*. It didn't take the children long to catch on to the pattern.

A is for trampoline.
B is for house.
C is for baby.

Why? Because the trampoline has acrobats.
Why? Because a house is built.
Why? Because a baby cries.

- The answers can be written upside down to surprise the next reader. The children are really fooling with the language, working with the concept, and building a whole new pattern.
- An alternative type of alphabet poem uses the alphabet to make a list poem, in this case, about the student's kitchen!

things found in my kitchen

apricots blades crap donuts eggs
freezer gingerale ham ice jam
knife lunch melon nuts ostrich meat
pork quiet relish spoon tablespoon
underwear on the floor!
vinegar water E<u>X</u>CEL gum
yolks zucchini

Josh

One, Two: A Poem for You

One, two,
Buckle my shoe;
Three, four,
Knock at the door;
Five, six,
Pick up sticks;
Seven, eight,
Lay them straight;
Nine, ten,
A big fat hen.

Eleven, twelve,
Dig and delve;
Thirteen, fourteen,
maids a-courting;
Fifteen, sixteen,
Maids in the kitchen;
Seventeen, eighteen,
Maids in waiting;
Nineteen, twenty,
My plate's empty.

The counting verse below is patterned on "One, One, Cinnamon Bun" by Clyde Watson. The teacher printed the students' ideas for the counting rhyme on chart paper, and they used this as material for choral reading. Then the children created illustrations for the story and published it in a book, *One, One, Elephants Come.* Your class can build a similar book, and share it with a younger grade.

One, one, elephants come,
two, two, kangaroo,
three, three, honeybee,
four, four, lions roar,
five, five, sea lions dive,
six, six, baby chicks,
seven, seven, a bear called Kevin,
eight, eight, monkeys wait,
nine, nine, porcupine,
ten, ten, start again.

Michael Rosen used a different number pattern for his poem below. You might have small groups or individual students work with only one number to build a poem.

The Motorbike

one bloke
one Suzuki
one cylinder
one spark plug
one journey
one a.m.
thousands driven crazeeeeee

A Poem by Numbers

Charles Causley's poem "One for the Man" is a good example of a counting poem with the shape and feel of the oral tradition.

> One for the man who lived by the sand,
> Two for his son and daughter,
> Three for the sea-birds washed so white
> That flew across the water.
>
> Four for the sails that brought the ship
> About the headland turning.
> Five for the jollyboys in her shrouds,
> Six for the sea-lamps burning.
>
> Seven for the sacks of silver and gold
> They sailed through the winter weather.
> Eight for the places set on shore
> When they sat down together.
>
> Nine for the songs they sang night-long,
> Ten for the candles shining.
> Eleven for the lawmen on the hill
> As they all were sweetly dining.
>
> Twelve for the hour that struck as they stood
> To the Judge so careful and clever.
> Twelve for the years that must come and go
> And we shall see them never.

- Speak the poem in unison.
- Start the piece with one solo voice, then add voices until everyone has contributed.
- Think about who is speaking the words to whom and why. Then, try reading the poem in role. (For example, are these the voices of children playing a game? the voices of longshoremen chanting as they load a ship? the voices of pirates? If so, how would it sound?)
- The surface of this poem is not the whole story. What questions do you have about the piece? What story is really being told?
- Do you think that the man and his family are innocent victims or are they up to no good?
- Work in pairs. Label yourselves A and B. Partner A plays a reporter investigating the story. Partner B is the judge who sentenced the man and his son and daughter. The reporter interviews the judge to get his understanding of the story.
- Can your class turn this poem into a song?

Calendar Patterns

"Thirty days hath September" is perhaps the best-known rhyme in the English language to help us remember facts. Can you find other examples of these types of verses? Perhaps you know of examples of rhymes to help people remember postal codes.

The following verses might have been devised to help us learn the days of the week. Cultural patterns that we find in days of the week, months of the year, and so on, are common in the old verses. You can collect examples of cultural patterns used by modern poets as well.

Solomon Grundy
Born on a Monday
Christened on Tuesday,
Married on Wednesday,
Took ill on Thursday,
Worse on Friday,
Died on Saturday,
Buried on Sunday.
This is the end of
Solomon Grundy.

Sneeze on Monday, sneeze for danger
Sneeze on Tuesday, kiss a stranger
Sneeze on Wednesday, get a letter
Sneeze on Thursday, something better
Sneeze on Friday, sneeze for sorrow
Sneeze on Saturday, see your sweetheart tomorrow.

• James, aged 11, uses the weekday pattern to build his "worry" poem. You can use his poem as a model for listing your own weekly concerns, using the days of the week as an organizing pattern. Or, you can borrow the pattern below right.

I worry a lot
Boy do I worry
On Mondays I worry
On Tuesdays I worry
On every day of the week
I worry
I worry about anything
and everything.

I'd like to be someone
who doesn't worry
Boy do I wish I didn't worry
Here I go again worrying
about worrying
I wish I didn't worry about
worrying about worrying.

James

On Monday, I worry about
_____;
On Tuesday, I worry about
_____;
On Wednesday, I worry about
_____;
On Thursday, I worry about
_____;
On Friday, I take the night off from worrying
and I _____ instead.
But on Saturday and Sunday,
The worrying returns.
And I want to stay in bed.

Seasonal Rhymes

The seasons offer us patterns for describing ideas, events, people, and places inside poem forms. The lines in the poems that follow are arranged month by month. You could try to write similar ones arranged by seasons or by decade. Web sites that chronicle or chart significant events for the year or decade might prove useful. In groups, consider using different time frames and locales for your poems. For example, you might choose the 1920s or focus on the North. Will you follow the pattern of one of the poems below?

The Months

January cold and desolate;
February dripping wet;
March wind ranges;
April changes;
Birds sing in tune
To flowers of May,
And sunny June
Brings longest day;
In scorched July
The storm clouds fly,
Lightning-torn;
August bears corn,
September fruit;
In rough October
Earth must disrobe her
Stars fall and shoot
In keen November;
And night is long
And cold is strong
In bleak December.

Christina Rossetti

The Months

January brings the snow,
Makes our feet and fingers glow.
February brings the rain,
Thaws the frozen lake again.
March brings breezes loud and shrill,
Stirs the dancing daffodil.
April brings the primrose sweet,
Scatters daisies at their feet.
May brings flocks of pretty lambs,
Skipping by their fleecy dams.
June brings tulips, lilies, roses,
Fills the children's hands with posies.
Hot July brings cooling showers,
Apricots and gillyflowers.
August brings the sheaves of corn,
Then the harvest home is borne.
Warm September brings the fruit,
Sportsmen then begin to shoot.
Fresh October brings the pheasant,
Then to gather nuts is pleasant.
Dull November brings the blast,
Then the leaves are whirling fast.
Chill December brings the sleet,
Blazing fire and Christmas treat.

Sara Coleridge

A List as a Poem

The list poem is a very old form of poetry that categorizes things or events. List poems can be of any length, rhymed or unrhymed.

Polynesian list poems formed an inventory of all the islands in Polynesia. In Book II of Homer's *Iliad*, the poet lists all the major Greek heroes who have come to fight in the Trojan War. In the Bible, the Book of Genesis can be seen as a list poem that traces the lineage of Adam's family.

- You can take an object, such as a potato, or an idea, such as transportation, and brainstorm all the parts that have to do with your topic. You can then arrange your bits and pieces into a poem. For example:

Boiled potato,
mashed potato
fried potato,
crisps
Jacket potato,
scalloped potato
puffed potato,
chips.

You can also turn the answer to a question into a list poem. The two list poems below each began with a question asked by a young poet.

Who is my baby brother?
  a gift from god
  a play buddy for me
  an extra family member
  the best thing that could ever happen
  a person who can make me happy . . .
    . . . even when I am sad
  a person who I can take care of
  the only thing that cheers me up
  the brightest star ever
  a one of a kind
  a friend
That's my baby brother!

Nathan

What is my country?
  a place where I was born
  a place strong and free
  where freedom is important
  a peaceful country
  justice for all
  where everyone is welcomed
  every culture everywhere
  a proud country
  my home and native land
  my protector
That is my country!

Matthew

A Simple Word Pattern

RimShots, a book by Charles R. Smith Jr., uses the phrase "I Remember." This pattern can help you tap into your memories. Once you have done so, plan to arrange your ideas into a poem, as the poet did in this tribute to basketball.

The class can choose a common theme, such as embarrassing moments, or you could select your own topic for an "I remember" poem.

Remembering Basketball Daze

I remember being so small that I wondered how I would ever get that big orange ball into that basket that seemed so high.

I remember beating my father at one-on-one after so many years.

I remember being the last one picked on my old street court.

I remember hitting the winning shot against the team that didn't pick me.

I remember learning how to play HORSE.

I remember my father regretting that he ever taught me the game after I beat him several times in a row.

I remember learning how to play with other kids.

I remember seeing Malik shake his defender to the ground so bad that the poor guy broke his ankle.

I remember running suicides in high school on the freshman team.

I remember showing up first and leaving last from practice.

I remember when I was the shortest on the team.

I remember the summer I grew tall enough to jump and touch the rim.

I remember challenging the star of the freshman team and beating him at one-on-one.

I remember playing with my cousins in Indiana from morning till night.

I remember when my dad could no longer play one-on-one.

I remember seeing my parents in the stands, even though I just played the bench.

I remember being called "big man" on the street courts.

I remember blocking my first shot.

I remember my first shot that was blocked.

I remember the day my mom took me to the 1985 NBA Championship Finals when Magic played for the Lakers and Dr. J played for the Philadelphia 76ers.

I remember going to Disneyland right after the championship game.

I remember practising free throws in the rain.

There are things I always forget, but when it comes to basketball, there are always many things that I remember.

Exploring Different Poetic Forms

Acrostics

Acrostic poetry is a form of short verse arranged so that the initial letters of each line taken consecutively form words. The basic acrostic is a poem in which the first letters of the lines, read downwards, form a word, phrase, or sentence. Acrostics are easy to write. First, you write vertically the word or phrase, then go back and fill out the lines, using as many words as you like.

Steven Schnur wrote acrostics in *Autumn: An Alphabet Acrostic*. Here's an example.

Teeth bared, they
Inch forward,
Growling softly,
Eager to
Reach the
Succulent zebra dinner.

- You can create similar poems about different animals, for example, zebras, rhinos, kittens, and snakes. Each sentence in the acrostic makes a statement about the animal, as in Steven Schnur's poem.

Soft skin
Quick runner
Unbelievably sharp claws
Interesting animal
Running fast
Running fast
Eating lots of nuts in their . . .
Lovely homes!

Milda

Frogs are
Really good swimmers.
Ontario creatures
Good hunters

Pretty in their own way
Ontario creatures
Never dry
Dew on the ground

Haley

- Try using a proverb, or wise saying, as the frame for an acrostic poem. Here is a sample proverb: People in glass houses shouldn't throw stones.

Haiku

Haiku began many years ago in Japan where poets wrote about common, everyday experiences, usually involving natural objects.

Haiku can be fun for you to use as the pattern for writing poems because it is short and has a clear shape. In haiku, every word counts.

There is no real recipe for haiku, but in North America, we often use 17 syllables divided into three lines of five, seven, and five syllables each. Lines are separated and each contains a new thought. Haiku is a very visual poetical format, leaving the reader with a clear, often delicate image that creates insight or emotion.

You can begin a haiku collection by finding and copying out ones you like from anthologies or Web sites. You can look through books about nature to find ideas for your own poems or tap into your memories of moments you want to capture.

Don't panic if you break the artificial rules of counting syllables. The point is for you to write something satisfying, not stick to a mathematical structure. You may also want to add a small drawing using a fine paintbrush and black paint, or a felt marker, to illuminate your poem. You can create a picture using words and images.

Now the swinging bridge
Is quieted with creepers
Like our tendrilled life

Basho

How reluctantly
the bee emerges from deep
within the peony

Basho

A world of dew,
and within every dewdrop
a world of struggle

Issa

Sunset coloured sky
Yellow to purple rainbow
Quickly becomes night

Blossom of pure snow
Crocus faces spring sunshine
Bright flower aglow

Weeping willows thrash
Autumn winds wildly howling
Sweet summer has passed

Julian

Limericks

There was an Old Man with a beard,
Who said, "It is just as I feared!
Two Owls and a Hen, four Larks and a Wren,
Have all built their nests in my beard!"

Born in 1812, Edward Lear has been called the Poet Laureate of the Limerick because of the mastery, wit, and humor that he brought to the form. His limericks have amused readers for 150 years. The simple verses about some very curious characters are as fresh and fun today as they were in 1846 when Lear's *Book of Nonsense* was published.

The English writer, whose best-known title is "The Owl and the Pussy-Cat," was also a talented painter of birds, animals, and landscapes. He gave drawing lessons to the long-ruling British monarch, Queen Victoria. He also illustrated his own limericks.

- For more on Edward Lear nonsense poems, check out http://edwardlear.tripod.com/.
- Lear's limericks make perfect simple scripts. You can dramatize them in small groups while reading the lines aloud. The more serious your voice sounds, the funnier the reading will be.

There was an Old Man who forgot,
That his tea was excessively hot.
When they said, "Let it cool,"
He answered, "You fool!
I shall pour it back into the pot."

There was a Young Lady whose eyes,
Were unique as to color and size;
When she opened them wide,
People all turned aside,
And started away in surprise.

There was an Old Man who supposed,
That the street door was partially closed;
But some very large rats,
Ate his coats and his hats,
While that futile old gentleman dozed.

There was a Young Lady, whose nose
Continually prospers and grows;
When it grew out of sight,
She exclaimed in a fright,
"Oh! Farewell to the end of my nose!"

- You can also find some contemporary limericks to use as models for writing around a theme. Arnold Lobel's *The Book of Pigericks* is full of new rhymes in old clothes.

There was a young pig whose delight
Was to follow the moths in their flight.
He entrapped them in nets,
Then admired his pets
As they danced on the ceiling at night.

Arnold Lobel

Jack Prelutsky's Rhyming Power

If Jack Prelutsky can't find the right word, he just makes one up!

Jack Prelutsky was born in Brooklyn and attended Hunter College in New York City. Although he claims to have once hated poetry, he rediscovered it and has devoted more than 20 years to writing about things that children really care about. He says, "I realized poetry was a means of communication, that it could be as exciting or as boring as that person or that experience."

After stints as a truck driver, photographer, folksinger, and more, he became the author of more than 30 collections of original, often humorous verse and anthologies of children's poetry. He now spends much of his time presenting poems to children in schools and libraries throughout North America.

What advice does he have for young writers? "READ! READ! READ! and WRITE! WRITE! WRITE!" he says. "Keep a notebook and write down things you see, hear, and think about. Ideas disappear quickly unless you jot them down. When you have an idea for a poem or story, write down anything you can think of that had to do with that idea. Study your list and you'll start to see connections among certain items. If you are writing poetry, don't force rhymes. It's better to work on what you want to say and create a feeling for the poem than to try to make up things just to make the poem rhyme."

Jack Prelutsky lives in Washington state with his wife, Carolyn.

The Dragons Are Singing Tonight

Tonight is the night all the dragons
Awake in their lairs underground
To sing in cacophonous chorus
And fill the whole world with their sound.
They sing of the days of their glory,
They sing of their exploits of old,
Of maidens and knights, and of fiery fights,
And guarding vast caches of gold.

Some of their voices are treble,
And some of their voices are deep,
But all of their voices are thunderous,
And no one can get any sleep.
I lie in my bed and I listen,
Enchanted and filled with delight,
To songs I can hear only one night a year —
The dragons are singing tonight.

It's Raining Pigs & Noodles, illustrated by James Stevenson
A Pizza the Size of the Sun, illustrated by James Stevenson
Something Big Has Been Here, illustrated by James Stevenson
New Kid on the Block, illustrated by James Stevenson
Monday's Troll, illustrated by Peter Sis
Tyrannosaurus Was a Beast: Dinosaur Poems, illustrated by Arnold Lobel
It's Valentine's Day, illustrated by Yossi Abolafia

CHAPTER 2

Poetry as Wordplay

Song of the Pop-Bottlers

Pop bottles pop-bottles
In pop shops;
The pop-bottles Pop bottles
Poor Pop drops.

When Pop drops pop-bottles,
Pop-bottles plop!
Pop-bottle-tops topple!
Pop mops slop!

Stop! Pop'll drop bottle!
Stop, Pop, stop!
When Pop bottles pop-bottles
Pop-bottles pop!

Morris Bishop

A sense of wordplay is common to all good poets. It's not that their works are always playful, but that they show a delight in the language, an awareness of its history and its feel, and a pleasure in what makes it sound effective in relation to what it means.

Poetry aims to open our ears to how words are used and to breathe life into words. By actively engaging in wordplay, children have an opportunity to develop a feeling for language and to discover how to look for the words that work best. By encouraging students to explore and experiment with words, poetry teaches them how to use language economically and powerfully. These are important discoveries that they can carry over into their own writing.

- They can play with the shapes, sounds, rhythms, and meaning of words as they read and write poems of all kinds.
- They can have word-play moments as breaks in classroom schedules. (Knock, knock. Who's there? Morris. Morris who? Morris Saturday ... Next day's Sunday.)
- They can record wordplay found in rhymes heard on the playground (Inty Pinty, Finkety Fell/ El dell dorman el/ Huckey puckey tarry rope/ On ton two's a joke/ You are out!)
- With your students, you can build a bulletin board featuring wordplay found in advertising. ("the winter supper warmer upper"—Ontario Veal; "Abba-Solutely Fab!—*Mamma Mia*) You can also have them collect sayings, for example, "Lie with dogs and you rise with fleas."
- Begin to collect language filled with wordplay: in the puns, jokes, tongue twisters, and riddles that are part of everyday life.
- Let students organize a word-play party, with only nonsense poems being shared, but in serious role-playing voices. For example, the poem "Song of the Pop-Bottlers" can be read as an important newscast on television, followed by an interview with Pop's children talking about him.
- Encourage students to find examples of poems with words gone from popular use or poems with "made-up" words in them.

Riddle Me a Rhyme

Old Mother Twitchett has but one eye,
And a long tail which she can let fly,
And every time she goes over a gap,
She leaves a bit of her tail in a trap.
(Answer: A needle and thread)

"Old Mother Twitchett" is a riddle which lays down concise clues in an imaginative way. Mother Goose is full of old riddles: for example, the riddle "White Bird Featherless" appears in Latin in the tenth century. Here is the English version:

White bird featherless,
Flew from paradise,
Pitched on the garden wall.
Along came Lord Landless,
Took it up handless,
And rode away horseless,
to the King's white hall.
(Answer: A snowflake)

- You can choose a common kitchen gadget or household item (e.g., scissors or pencil with an eraser on the end) and try to disguise it in the form of a riddle. There may be more than one suitable answer as students read their riddles aloud.

What force or strength cannot get through
I, with gentle touch, can do;
And many in the street could stand,
Were I not, as a friend, at hand.
(Answer: A key)

- Create a "riddle centre" in your classroom, where you and the students bring in books of riddles. Play a game, Stump the Riddler. Who can answer the most riddles before being defeated?
- The riddles on the next page can be written on cards and used as a reading comprehension game where, in groups, students attempt to find an answer for each one. You can read the traditional answers aloud when everyone has completed reading the cards.

Answers: 1. Fire; 2. Peace; 3. A ring; 4. A medicine bottle; 5. A drum; 6. A kite; 7. A flea; 8. Ants; 9. A worm; 10. Bees making honey; 11. A sloth; 12. An orange.

Riddles for the Answering

1. The more you feed it,
   The more it'll grow high;
   But if you give it water
   It'll go and die.

2. My first is in apple and also in pear,
   My second's in desperate and also in dare,
   My third is in sparrow and also in lark,
   My fourth is in cashier and also in clerk,
   My fifth is in seven and also in ten,
   My whole is a blessing indeed unto men.

3. The King of Cumberland
   Gave the Queen of Northumberland
   A bottomless vessel
   To put flesh and blood in.

4. He wears his hat upon his neck
   Because he has no head,
   And he never takes his hat off
   Until you're sick in bed.

5. My sides are firmly laced about,
   Yet nothing is within;
   You'll think my head is strange indeed,
   Being nothing else but skin.

6. My body is thin,
   And has no guts within,
   I have neither head, face, nor eye,
   But a tail I have got,
   As long as—what not,
   And without any wings I can fly.

7. What loves a dog
   And rides on his back,
   Travels for miles
   And leaves not a track?

8. Once I was going up the hipple steeple,
   I met a crowd of little people,
   Some were red and some were black,
   Some were the color of gingersnaps!

9. Long man legless
   Came to the door staffless,
   More afraid of a rooster and hen
   Than he was of a dog and ten men.

10. Behind the king's kitchen there is a great vat,
    And a great many workmen working at that.
    Yellow are their toes, yellow are their clothes.
    Tell me this riddle and you can pull my nose.

11. Lives in a forest far away
    To climb down a tree it takes all day
    Its moss covered body is black and grey
    When you want to guess it'll take you a day.

    Callum

12. It is round
    It is juicy
    You can drink it when it's squeezed.

    Emily

Riddling: A Demonstration

This activity is modelled on work by poet Kevin Crossley-Holland. Try developing a riddle together as a class. Choose a common household object and place it where all the students can see it. For this demonstration, a salt grinder was used.

Teacher: What can you tell me about this salt grinder?

Student: It's shaped like a tube.

Teacher: Anything else?

Student: You hold it in your hand.

Teacher: Good, so we have a hand-held tube. Can you tell me how it works?

Student: You twist the top.

Teacher: Can you think of another word for top that paints a more exact picture?

Student: Maybe the head.

Teacher: All right. We twist the head of a hand-held tube. Why do we twist it?

Student: Because that grinds the salt.

Teacher: Let's see if we can use another word for salt that is not so obvious. How would you describe the salt?

Student: They're like little crystals. When they come out of the bottom, it's like rain.

Teacher: Good. How else could we describe it?

Student: Maybe the salt is crying.

Teacher: So, we have a hand-held tube that cries when you twist its head. Do the tears go anywhere?

Student: On your food.

Teacher: Let's see what we've got:

Twist the head of this hand-held tube
And it weeps crystals on your food.
What is it?

There, we've just made a riddle.

From Sounds into Poetry

Many poets fill their poems with the sounds of language. It is not easy to make a reader hear the very sounds being described, but poets enjoy trying, and often, they are quite successful.

- What words could you invent to describe these sounds:

  - yawning
  - talking with your mouth full
  - undoing a Velcro strap
  - squishing a paper bag

- What is happening in the following scene? Bring the scene to life using sound words only.

Clip clop
Clip clop
Clip clop, clip clop
Clip clop, clip clop
Clip clop, clip clop clip clop, clip clop
Clip clop, clip clop clip clop, clip clop
Clippety clop clippetty clap
Clippety cloppetty, clippetty cloppetty

- List some tools that a carpenter might use. Examples are hammers and saws. Create the sound of a tool in written words, and see if your classmates can match the word to the sound.

- Gather the names of wild creatures and put them together to make interesting sounds and a pleasing rhythm. Below is an example.

Kangaroo Octopus
Mosquito Hippopotamus
Baboon Rhinoceros
Porcupine Snail

- You can make other interesting sound patterns using groupings of tree, flower, automobile, or boat names. For example, here are some boat names: kayak, canoe, catamaran, junk

Kayak, canoe, catamaran, junk,
One was made from a great tree trunk.

The Sound of Words: A Demonstration

In one Grade 2 class with a large English as a Second Language population, the teacher introduced her students to Henry Newbolt's poem "Night Is Come."

> Night is come
> Owls are out;
> Beetles hum
> Round about.
> Children snore
> Safe in bed.
> Nothing more
> Need be said.

Before looking at the poem, the teacher asked the students to close their eyes and listen to all the sounds inside the classroom, then all the sounds outside the classroom. After the sounds had been inventoried and discussed, the teacher asked the students to close their eyes again." The teacher tapped a pencil on the edge of a book a few times. "What could be making this sound?" she asked.

The teacher reported that when students opened their eyes and gave ideas, most tried to guess how she had made the sound. It took a few tries for her to get them to use their imaginations instead. Scratching her fingernails over the surface of a tambourine and crumpling pieces of paper in her hand finally triggered imaginative responses. The teacher now introduced the poem by asking the students to listen for some night sounds that the poet had identified. The students discussed the actual sounds that the poet heard and also sounds that were hinted at. Using an overhead projector, the teacher showed the poem to the class and they read it in unison. Next, the students alternated the reading, half the class reading one line, the other half the next. When the teacher asked for soloists to read specific lines, response was enthusiastic. Even the least confident readers could manage these simple lines.

Together, the class discussed the short lines and why they thought the poet wrote them like that. They questioned the line "Beetles hum." If beetles don't hum, why did the poem say that? Finally, the teacher got the class talking about lullabies, and they invented a tune and sang the poem as it might be sung to help a baby sleep.

The teacher then asked the students to think of three sounds they have heard in the night at home in their beds. "What," she asked, "do the sounds remind you of? When you hear them, how do you feel?"

Next, the class discussed the shape of Newbolt's poem and how it was really a list. The students were challenged to shape a piece in this fashion. A student named Sara wrote "The Sounds in My Apartment," below.

> I hear a cricket singing Crick, crick, crick.
> I hear the clock ticking Tick, tick, tick.
> I hear my mom wash dishes Swish, swish, swish.
> I hear my window Swing, swing, swing.

Rhymes and Jingles from the Playground

Vegetable Love,
Do you carrot all for me?
My heart beets for you.
With your turnip nose
And your radish face,
You are a peach.
If we cantaloupe,
Lettuce marry;
Weed make a swell pear.

At play, we can hear children calling out skipping rhymes, jingles, riddles, sayings, superstitions, taunts and teases, cat-calls and retorts, autograph verses, street songs, counting-out rhymes, ball-bounce chants, tongue twisters, join-in rhythms, action songs, nonsense verses, lullabies, jokes, silly rhymes, parodies, nicknames, slogans, and ads, all shouted and sung in the freedom of the playground. These verses form the folk poetry of childhood. We may recognize a phrase from a television show, a tune from an advertisement, a line from a cartoon, a rhyme from a song; there may be a rude expression for an enemy, a city with an interesting-sounding name, an alphabet rhyme for choosing who is first, a counting verse for deciding who was last, a friend's name made into a rhyme. Like magic, these creations alter overnight, springing up anew on an unsuspecting playground in some other city.

All these old chants and verses that we seem to dredge up from early memories to pass on to our children are the rags and bones of a once flourishing oral tradition of folklore and song, one that our newer print-soaked society has driven underground or transformed into television jingles and other kinds of popular culture.

For teachers, these "other nursery rhymes" written on the streets and playgrounds of urban centres, free from adult interference, can provide an important bridge between the students and the poetry of books and school.

- Let children fill a bulletin board with rhymes and jingles that they have overheard on the playground or been exposed to by television.
- How many rhyming ads can they record? Suggest that they see whether parents have verses to contribute.
- Invite students to search for Web sites featuring street rhymes from other locales. Let students compare these rhymes with their own.
- How many skipping rhymes do they know? They can check older versions in anthologies such as *Dr. Knickerbocker* by David Booth.
- What fan cheers for different sports teams do they know? Invite the children to share their favorite team cheers.

Foolies in the Playground

- How many ways can you say these rhymes aloud? You might put yourselves in the shoes of football cheerleaders, demonstration participants, rock video performers, and more.

Piggy on the railway, picking up stones, Up came an engine and broke Piggy's bones. "Oh!" said Piggy, "that's not fair." "Oh!" said the driver, "I don't care."	A wise old owl lived in an oak; The more he saw, the less he spoke; The less he spoke, the more he heard. Why aren't we all like that wise old bird?
Nellie Bligh caught a fly Going home from school, Put it in a hot mince pie Waiting by to cool.	Grandpa Grig had a pig, In a field of clover; Piggie died, Grandpa cried, And all the fun was over.
Higglety, pigglety, pop! The dog has eaten the mop; The pig's in a hurry, The cat's in a flurry Higglety, pigglety, pop!	Inky pinky ponky Daddy bought a donkey Donkey died, Daddy cried, Inky pinky ponky.
Moses supposes his toeses are roses, But Moses supposes erroneously. For Moses he knowses his toeses aren't roses, As Moses supposes his toeses to be.	Salome was a dancer, She danced before the king. She danced the hanky-panky, And she shimmied everything. The king said, "Salome, You can't do that in here!" Salome said, "Baloney!" And kicked the chandelier.

Old John Tucker was a mighty man,
He washed his face in a frying pan,
He combed his hair with a wagon wheel,
And had a toothache in his heel.
So get out of the way, old John Tucker,
You're too late to get your supper.
	The funniest thing I've ever seen
	Was a tomcat sewing on a sewing machine.
	Oh, the sewing machine got running too
	    slow,
	And it took seven stitches in the tomcat's
	    toe.

Tongue Twister Poems

Tongue twisters twist tongues twisted
Trying to untangle twisted tangles:
My tang's tungled now.

Tongue twisters are meant to be spoken aloud quickly, repeatedly, and as accurately as possible. Pick an appealing one and learn it by heart. Who can set the record for the most rapid-fire recitations in a row before stumbling? Can you turn a tongue twister into a script for reading aloud? Take up the challenge!

Three grey geese in the green grass grazing, Grey were the geese, and green was the grazing.	**Say!** Say, did you say, or did you not say What I said you said? For it is said that you said That you did not say What I said you said. Now if you say that you did not say What I said you said, Then what do you say you did say instead Of what I said you said?
Swan swam over the sea, Swim, swan, swim! Swan swam back again, Well swum swan!	
Three little ghostesses, Sitting on postesses, Eating buttered toastesses, Greasing their fistesses, Up to their wristesses, Oh, what beastesses To make such feastesses!	Robert Rowley rolled a round roll round, A round roll Robert Rowley rolled round; Where rolled the round roll Robert Rowley rolled round?
Once upon a barren moor There dwelt a bear, also a boar; The bear could not bear the boar; The boar thought the bear a bore. At last the boar could bear no more The bear that bored him on the moor; And so one morn the bear he bored The bear will bore the boar no more.	Said she to me, "Was that you?" Said I, "Who?" Said she, "You." Said I, "Where?" Said she, "There." Said I, "When?" Said she, "Then." Said I, "No." Said she, "Oh ..."

Still Twisting Those Tongues

Poets today still love using words that tickle our tongues and our funny bones.

- Create a collection of poems by contemporary poets who find words that trick our eyes and confuse our lips. You might look for other poems by the poets represented below.

I Like It When It's Mizzly

I like it when it's mizzly
and just a little drizzly
so everything looks far away
and make-believe and frizzly.

I like it when it's foggy
and sounding very froggy,
I even like it when it rains
on streets and weepy windowpanes
and catkins in the poplar tree
and *me*.

Aileen Fisher

I saveth! saith the sloth
I am slow because
That's the way it is
The way it was
My three toes doth
What three toes do
I'm as happy for me
As you are for you
And the wayeth the world
Spinneth upside down?
It's just different, not weird
My sky is your ground
And if-eth you thinketh
That faster is better
I sayeth to you
That it doesn't much matter
For if you're a sloth
Slow seemeth just fine
You doeth things your way
I'll doeth things mine.

Sheree Fitch

The Muddy Puddle

I am sitting
In the middle
Of a rather Muddy
Puddle,
With my bottom
Full of bubbles
And my rubbers
Full of Mud,

While my jacket
And my sweater
Go on slowly
Getting wetter
As I very
Slowly settle
To the Bottom
Of the Mud.

And I find that
What a person
With a puddle
Round his middle
Thinks of mostly
In the muddle
Is the Muddiness of Mud.

Dennis Lee

Creating Words

A Demonstration

Poet Diane Dawber leads a workshop in which she gets students telling stories about playing or fooling around with family or friends. She might get things started by asking, "Have you ever gotten up high to see more—up on your dad's shoulders, up a tree, on a fence?" "Who do you like to wrestle with?" "Has anyone ever wrestled with a bird?"

After the students share personal experiences, she often reads some poems chronicling similar events. Here is one she wrote:

Knocking the Wind Out

Such a big log
not very long
but high as my waist
so I lean on it
lovely and warm from the sun.
How much better to sit so
I climb on
so smooth, no bark
so round, so high ...
I bet I'll set a lot
if I stand.
I can!
This must be the way my dad sees.

What was that?
A wobble?
Never!
A log like this is solid as a rock
in a creek.
OOOFF!

Now that the world
my voice
and my breath
have started again
I can tell you
it's scary
having them stop.

Diane now has the students write in response to this question: "Ever fall or have the wind knocked out of you?" She has them answer these questions with phrases:

* Where are you?
* Who is there?
* What are you doing?
* What sound happens?

Students then create a new sound expression and invent its spelling. One student wrote:

In my bedroom
me and my cousin
bounced on the bed
BABONK!
Heads throb, throb, throb.

Much of the fun reading the pieces aloud comes in how the students give voices to their newly minted onomatopoeic words.

Diane Dawber's Snow Fleas

Diane Dawber writes poetry near Kingston, Ontario. She is always looking for the unexplained because mystery is where poems live and children too. She spends some of her non-writing time helping others find more ease and delight in writing and teaching poetry. She believes most people needn't worry about complicated poetic vocabulary.

"In any poem, it is a great deal to talk about the picture, the sound, and the relation of the poem to our own experiences," she says. "Sometimes, when you are writing a poem, it becomes necessary to identify what is producing the effect or blocking it, and more technical terms may be required. The mechanic needs to know about the tie rod ends, but the driver may need to know only that the steering seems off."

Looking for Snow Fleas

I'm looking for
      springtails
            snow fleas
                  black dots on white
jumping
and just as I exclaim
"Look! I've found them! Snow fleas!"
a lady walks by with her dog.

"Oh no!" she says
yanking the dog's leash.
"I don't want my dog to catch snow fleas."

"It's okay," I say
"They don't like dogs."

She still looks alarmed.

"Or people either.
They just eat stuff in the snow."

"Cool," say two kids in snowsuits.

"Cool," says an old guy on skis.

"And look.
They can't even jump out of a deep footprint.
The bottom is grey with them."

I admire the tiny black bodies
cozying up to the cold.
Nothing cooler than snow fleas

My Cake's on Fire!
How Do You Wrestle a Goldfish?
My Underwear's Inside Out
Oatmeal Mittens

CHAPTER 3

Mother Goose's Family

Cackle cackle, Mother Goose
Have you any feathers loose?
Truly have I pretty fellow
Half enough to fill a pillow
Here are quills, take one or
   two,
And down to make a bed for
   you.

For many years, Mother Goose has played a huge role in our work in schools. Since a lot of the traditional nursery rhymes were unfamiliar to some children, we wanted to let them feel the rhythms and try on the words as pleasurably as possible. Although archaic words and expressions and odd vocabulary fill the rhymes, we found that they seldom pose any barriers to the children's delight and understanding. The nursery rhymes create powerful and evocative images and feature characters that stay with us throughout our lives. The stories that the rhymes tell (or hint at) are rich with possibilities for the children's own storymaking, at any age, in any grade.

We delight in discovering with children the unknown verses, chants, calls, and lullabies that need voices to bring them to life. And in response the children can write their own poems, tell their own stories, and paint their own pictures stimulated by the lore of Mother Goose.

Baa Baa black sheep
Have you any wool?
Yes, sir, Yes, sir,
Three bags full.
One for the master
And one for the dame
And one for the little boy
Who lives down the lane.

England wouldn't permit the export of wool from the country as raw wool, but insisted on selling it as piece goods. The weavers in the cottages tried to save as much of the wool for themselves as possible by stretching the material and providing a certain length without using all of the raw wool. The one bag for the master is that woven into material, and the one bag for the dame was the amount saved by fraudulent means. In 1275 an export tax was imposed on wool, so the one bag for the little boy who lives down the lane was the amount needed to pay the tax collector. At that time black sheep were much sought after, as it was possible to make black stockings without dying the yarn. So the masters were accused of trying to keep all the black wool for themselves.

Jean Harrowven in *Origins of Rhymes, Songs and Sayings*

How the Rhymes Began

One of the best-known poems in the English language was written by Jane Taylor and appeared in *Rhymes for the Nursery* in 1806.

Twinkle, Twinkle, Little Star

Twinkle, twinkle, little star,
How I wonder what you are!
Up above the world so high,
Like a diamond in the sky.

When the blazing sun is gone,
When he nothing shines upon,
Then you show your little light,
Twinkle, twinkle, all the night.

Then the traveller in the dark,
Thanks you for your tiny spark,
He could not see which way to go,
If you did not twinkle so.

In the dark blue sky you keep,
And often through my curtains peep,
For you never shut your eye,
Till the sun is in the sky.

As your bright and tiny spark,
Lights the traveller in the dark—
Though I know not what you are,
Twinkle, twinkle, little star.

If ever a rhyme cried out for parody, surely it is this one. A parody is a humorous, exaggerated imitation. "Twinkle, Twinkle, Little Star" has been frequently parodied, as in the Mad Hatter's song by Lewis Carroll in *Alice in Wonderland*.

Twinkle, twinkle, little bat!
How I wonder what you're at!
Up above the world you fly,
Like a tea tray in the sky.

• This poem offers you a simple pattern to begin with as you explore rhythm and rhyme. Model a poem on this 200-year-old verse.

Taking a Feather from Mother Goose

In the nursery rhymes by Caribbean poets John Agard and Grace Nichols, we find a fresh alternative to traditional collections. The pair from Guyana moved to Britain in 1977. They looked at the familiar nursery rhymes and created a host of entirely original rhymes and characters. Here is a poem by John Agard:

> Pumpkin
> Pumpkin
> Where have you been?
>
> I been to hallowe'en
> to frighten the queen
>
> Pumpkin
> Pumpkin
> how did you do it?
>
> With two holes for my eyes
> and a light
> in me head
> I frightened the queen
> right under her bed!

Poets have always felt the power of Mother Goose. Kate Greenaway's lines echo the qualities of the nursery rhymes perfectly.

> Little wind, blow on the hilltop;
> Little wind, blow down the plain;
> Little wind, blow up the sunshine;
> Little wind, blow off the rain.

Like nursery rhymes, much of contemporary light verse for children skirts the forbidden and the taboo. Anarchy, titillation, and the risqué counterpoint feeling and sentiment. Wordplay is a big part of this type of poetry—puns, tongue twisters, scrambled words, and near-rhyme. Colloquial rhymes, the rhythms of the speaking voice, the storytelling quality, along with the subjects of a child's life, make these new poems accessible to children and introduce poetry as a natural phenomenon.

> Sing a song of soapsuds
> Filling up the sink
> Five & five a-washing
> Quick as a wink
>
> When the water's dirty
> Send it down the drain
> Curlie-wurlie, there it goes
> & shan't be seen again
>
> *Clyde and Wendy Watson*

Today's poets have often taken the well-known rhymes, the slapstick humor, the wit, and the comic spirit of Mother Goose and borrowed them for their own writing. The best of them, such as Dennis Lee, Jack Prelutsky, Sheree Fitch, Eve Merriam, and Shel Silverstein, create simple, yet clever verse incorporating new ideas and the rhythms of Mother Goose. These poets use sound patterns that have the rhymes of the poems of long ago and the rhythms that helped them to be remembered.

Eve Merriam created *Inner City Mother Goose*, a parody of the rhymes. Here's an example:

> One misty moisty morning,
> Virus was the weather;
> Waiting for the bus to come,
> Closed in together.
>
> One began to cough and shake,
> Another cursed his mother,
> Someone swiped a wallet;
> A day like any other.

- You might involve your class in creating your own Inner City Mother Goose. Students could produce collages from pictures in magazines and newspapers, or download images from Web sites. The class could make a large mural that shows the contrasts between yesteryear and today.

Other nursery rhymes and lullabies were collected from immigrants. They were passed on from generation to generation by mothers, fathers, and other family members who heard them as children and later sang them to their own children.

- Invite children to collect rhymes from around the world from families and neighbors. Perhaps the speakers could tape-record the rhymes and the tapes could be brought to class.

Duérmete mi niña,	Sleep, my child,
Duérmete mi sol,	Sleep, my sun,
Duérmete pedazo	Sleep, little piece
De mi corazón	Of my heart.
(*Arrulle al niño para que se duerma.*)	(*Rock the child to sleep.*)

Rearranging the Rhymes

This activity will help you to explore shaping a poem and thinking about the words. The poem "The Park" was cut up into words and phrases, and two students created the new version beside it by rearranging the words.

The Park

I'm glad that I
Live near a park

For in the winter
After dark

The park lights shine
As bright and still

As dandelions
On a hill.

James S. Tippett

On a hill
In a winter park
That I live near
(After dark)
The park lights shine
As dandelions
Still and bright
And
I'm glad.

James and Sarah

- The individual lines of a poem need to be cut up into a pile for each group.
- In groups of four, create a poem using the words in whatever order or sequence pleases you. Listen to the sounds of your piece by reading it aloud as it takes shape.
- Remember that exploring sounds and patterns of sounds is more important than finding the right answer.
- When you are satisfied with your arrangement, decide how the group will read the poem aloud.
- After the out-loud readings, explain how you arrived at your final pattern. Where did you have difficulty agreeing and why were you satisfied with the end product?
- Look at the poem in its original form. How does your version compare with the original? Which do you prefer?

Note: The best way to play this rearranging game is by not reading the original poem until you have created your own.

Dennis Lee's Irresistible Pie

Dennis Lee was born in Toronto, Ontario. His first poem was published in a children's magazine when he was only seven. An avid reader as a child, he says that when he liked a book, he would "live inside it" until he finished reading it.

Dennis graduated with B.A. and M.A. degrees in English Literature from the University of Toronto. He considered many careers before teaching at the university level for eight years.

When Dennis's children were young, he began composing chants and rhymes for children, especially with Canadian content. He felt it was important that Canadian children develop a sense of their Canadian identity, and he wanted to share his excitement over the huge shifts in the ethnic diversity of the country's population. Eventually this poetry was published in two books: *Alligator Pie*, winner of the 1974 IODE Book Award—Toronto chapter and the 1975 Canadian Library Association Book of the Year Award for Children, and *Nicholas Knock and Other People*. Dennis's *Garbage Delight* (1977) won the 1978 Canadian Library Association Book of the Year Award for Children and the 1978 Ruth Schwartz Children's Book Award. In 1994, Dennis was awarded the Order of Canada.

"A poem enacts in words the presence of what we live among. It arises from the tough, delicate, heartbreaking rooting of what is in its own nonbeing," he says. "From that rooting, there arise elemental movements of being: of hunger, of play, of rage, of celebration, of dying. Such movements are always particular, speaking the things which are. A poem enacts those living movements in words."

If I could teach you how to fly
Or bake an elderberry pie
Or turn the sidewalk into stars
Or play new songs on an old guitar
Or if I knew the way to heaven,
The names of night, the taste of seven
And owned them all, to keep or lend—
Would you come and be my friend?

You cannot teach me how to fly.
I love the berries but not the pie.
The sidewalks are for walking on,
And an old guitar has just one song.
The names of night cannot be known,
The way to heaven cannot be shown.
You cannot keep, you cannot lend
But I still want you for my friend.

The Ice Cream Store, illustrated by David McPhail
The Dennis Lee Big Book, illustrated by Barbara Klunder
Jelly Belly, illustrated by Juan Wijngaard
The Ordinary Bath, illustrated by Jon McKee
Garbage Delight, illustrated by Frank Newfeld
Alligator Pie, illustrated by Frank Newfeld
Nicholas Knock and Other People, illustrated by Frank Newfeld

CHAPTER 4

Painting Images with Words

Millions of Strawberries

Marcia and I went over the
  curve,
Eating our way down
Jewels of strawberries we
  didn't deserve,
Eating our way down.
Till our hands were sticky, and
  our lips painted,
And over us the hot day
  fainted,
And we saw snakes,
And got scratched,
And a lust overcame us for the
  red unmatched
Small buds of berries,
Till we lay down—
Eating our way down—
And rolled in the berries like
  two little dogs,
Rolled
In the late gold.
And gnats hummed,
And it was cold,
And home we went, home
  without a berry,
Painted red and brown,
Eating our way down.

Genevieve Taggard

Poets take photographs of our country, our seasons, our weather, our people and us without camera or film. You may find yourself in the photo albums created by poets. Savor the poems, feel them, wonder about them, and find some more of them. Reread them if you want to. Say them aloud. Read one to a friend. Laugh if you feel like it. Forget some of them. Memorize some of them. Don't pick them apart—that hurts a poem. Copy down the ones you enjoy the most. Leave out the ones you don't understand or don't like. (Come back to them later; give them a second chance.) Write your own poems. People who read poems often want to write them. If a poet connects with you, read a whole book by that poet. The poem "Millions of Strawberries" paints such a vivid picture of this red fruit that we can almost taste them.

Part of the fun of exploring a variety of collections is discovering the ways in which different illustrators have tried to entice the viewer to look again at something familiar. With a large body of poems to choose from, what lies behind the decisions to select certain ones and why have they been juxtaposed in a certain fashion? For example, consider the challenge of illustrating this:

> When I was a little boy,
> I washed my mammy's dishes;
> I put my finger in my eye
> And pulled out golden fishes.

Any attempt to translate the literal truth into images would be unwelcome at best. To dodge the piece by showing, as some have, a boy staring at the tip of his index finger or a boy bending over and scrubbing a large plate falls far short of the mark. Illustrator Dan Jones dealt with this verse in *Mother Goose Comes to Gable Street*. He drew a boy at a kitchen sink holding a glass plate, then filled the space around him with soap bubbles. One large bubble floats at the boy's eye level and two golden fishes formed from the reflection of an electric light bulb stare out. How would your students attempt to create visual meanings with this particular poem puzzle?

Seeing Poems as Pictures

Poetry and art often go together. Once students read the poem "Lemon Moon," they could illustrate it using different art forms: magazine pictures, drawings, paintings, or computer art. You could then display the illustrations in a "poetry gallery" to demonstrate how different artists have different interpretations of the same poem.

Students could write poems in special shapes, just as Sarah did with her poem, "Snail Tale," and Natasha with "My Poem." They could also use calligraphy or an artistic computer font to present their poems.

Natasha

Lemon Moon

On a hot and thirsty summer night,
The moon's a wedge of lemon light
Sitting low among the trees,
Close enough for you to squeeze
And make a moonade, icy-sweet,
To cool your summer-dusty heat.

Beverly McLoughland

Sara

Building an Anthology

A Demonstration

Students can create their own poetry anthologies based on patterns of organization that appeal to them. Whether the rhymes are gathered by subject (cats, work, eating), type (tongue twisters, riddles, game rhymes), theme (big and little, wise and foolish), pattern of discourse (conversations, declarations, exclamations) or any other possibilities the students find for juxtaposing the selections, some exciting discoveries can be made:

- Students can classify poems by the opinions represented. They can arrange poems by viewpoint, attitude, behavior, religion, ethics, and morality.
- They can translate the form of the poem into other types of writing, for example, monologues, scripts, or vice versa. They need to find rhymes that link together in some way.
- They could examine picture books such as *Michael Foreman's Mother Goose* to gain many ideas for layout and design. After reading the poems, students could explain the words they liked, the way the words made them feel, and how the words sounded special. These responses can be put on a chart and categorized and classified. The students can list their favorite words and phrases, the rhymes they enjoy, the pictures they think are best, the metaphors and the comparisons they will remember. Students may want to draft their own questions about the poems and make these the focus of group work or class discussion. They may jot down their thoughts and feelings as they are reading each poem, almost in a stream of consciousness with associations, connotations, and reflections.
- Once collections have been assembled, the students can concentrate on what images, thoughts, and feelings pass through their minds or what memories are triggered by the assemblages. Images and words torn from magazines can then be put into collages to illustrate the anthologies. Some students may prefer to explore sound collages, arranging their anthologies for oral performance by solo and chorus voices.
- A menagerie of creatures could be the stimulus for a collection of rhymes drawn from several classroom anthologies. These could be depicted on a display board or in a large class book: snails, cows, robins, frogs, foxes, flies, dogs, cats, donkeys, and roosters.
- Different groups that have explored various aspects of a theme or topic in the rhymes may want to hear from other groups to expand their knowledge. They can transfer their findings to scripts, overhead transparencies, or large charts and share the information.
- You can share a poem without a title. The students can then decide on an appropriate or possible title after rereading the poem. Titles can be suggested, discussed, and voted upon.

Going Beyond the Snapshots

Nursery rhymes still feature some lively females, who do their own work, disobey some of the rules, and are not always as easily married off as their critics have sometimes implied. They offer a lively and occasionally outspoken commentary on the male-female relationship in many of its aspects, often more vividly than is the case in other kinds of children's literature.

Nicholas Tucker

How can we explore the snapshots of the lives of the women captured in old rhymes? As Nicholas Tucker has suggested, many of these female characters have survived under terrible circumstances. Students may try to fill in the missing pieces of the puzzles through discussion, role-play, painting, or storytelling.

- Form small groups. Consider the questions below as you look at a particular rhyme. A sample appears below.

  A famous old woman was Madam McBight,
  She slept all day, she slept all night,
  One hour was given to victuals and drink
  And only a minute was taken to think.

  How could the woman in the rhyme have arrived at her present situation?
  What went wrong or right along the way?
  What obstacles did she overcome?
  Did any difficulties overwhelm her?
  What stories could she now tell? Does she?
  What other tales do people tell about her?
  Where does she live now? Does she own anything?
  Does she dream of changing her life, or has she accepted her situation?
  At a community function—a wedding or a funeral—does she take part?
  Does she have any special friends?
  Do strangers seek her out?

- Groups can share their stories about these women from the rhymes and look for similarities and differences between them. To learn about a woman's life, perhaps one group could question a member of another group who answers in role as the woman in question.
- Develop your own stories from one of the stories heard or read. This activity is called "versioning." You can determine place, time, characters, details, mood, style, and technique.
- You can create visual timelines to represent these poems. For example, you might draw incidents in a poem and hang pictures on a clothesline in the sequence in which the events occurred.
- You can also magnify one small detail or incident in your story and prepare a close-up view of your vision of it. You might focus on a scene briefly mentioned, a place not described, or an incident only referred to.

Long Ago Women

Here's a poor widow from Babylon,
With six poor children all alone;
One can bake, and one can brew,
One can shape, and one can sew,
One can sit at the fire and spin,
One can bake a cake for the king;
    Come choose you east,
    Come choose you west,
    Come choose the one
    You love the best.

There was an old woman, and what do you think?
She lived upon nothing but victuals and drink:
Victuals and drink were the chief of her diet;
And yet this old woman could never keep quiet.

She went to the baker, to buy her some bread,
And when she came home, her old husband was
    dead;
She went to the clerk to toll the bell,
And when she came back her old husband was
    well.

There was an old woman of Surrey,
Who was morn, noon, and night in a
    hurry;
Called her husband a fool,
Drove her children to school,
The worrying old woman of Surrey.

There was an old woman of Norwich,
Who lived upon nothing but
    porridge;
Parading into town,
She turned cloak into gown,
The thrifty old woman of Norwich.

The old woman must stand
    At the tub, tub, tub,
The dirty clothes
    To rub, rub, rub;
But when they are clean
    And fit to be seen,
She'll dress like a lady,
    And dance on the green.

There was an old woman
Liv'd under a hill,
And if she isn't gone,
She lives there still.

Baked apples she sold,
And cranberry pies,
And she's the old woman
That never told lies.

There was an old woman
    and nothing she had,
And so this old woman
    Was said to be mad.
She'd nothing to eat,
    She'd nothing to wear,
She'd nothing to lose,
    She'd nothing to fear,
She'd nothing to ask,
    And nothing to give,
And when she did die
    She'd nothing to leave.

There was an old woman
    who lived in Dundee,
And in her back garden
    There grew a plum tree;

The plums they grew rotten
    Before they grew ripe,
And she sold them
    Three farthings a pint.

James Berry's Nest Full of Stars

James Berry was born in Jamaica and grew up in a village on the coast. When he was 17, he went to the United States, but stayed only four years as he hated the way black people were treated. He returned to his home village, but finding it claustrophobic, immigrated to Britain in 1948. He now lives in Brighton and visits Jamaica frequently. He is a leading campaigner for black people and helps young black writers.

"I experienced the West Indies and myself in it as a hidden-away place and person," he writes. "When I grew up there, we never had anything like a 'Caribbean poem' or story that showed us something about ourselves and our way of life. Our poems and stories all came from the U.K. [United Kingdom] and celebrated that way of life. Now, some of my poems and stories try to contribute school material, for both the U.K. and the Caribbean, which never existed in my days at school."

Hurricane

Under low black clouds
the wind was all
speedy feet, all horns and breath,
all bangs, howls, rattles,
in every hen house,
church hall and school.

Roaring, screaming, returning,
it made forced entry, shoved walls,
made rifts, brought roofs down,
hitting rooms to sticks apart.

It wrung soft banana trees,
broke tough trunks of palms.
It pounded vines of yams,
left fields battered up.

Invisible with such ecstasy
with no intervention of sun or man —
everywhere kept changing branches.

Zinc sheets are kites.
Leaves are panic swarms.
Fowls are fixed with feathers turned.
Goats, dogs, pigs,
all are people together.

Then growling it slunk away
from muddy, mossy trail and boats
in hedges and cows, ratbats, trees,
fish, all dead in the road.

James Berry

Classic Poems to Read Aloud
Around the World in Eighty Poems (with Katherine Lucas)
When I Dance: Poems (with Karen Barbour and Bonnie V. Ingber)
A Nest Full of Stars (with Ashley Bryan)
A Thief in the Village and Other Stories
Celebration Song: A Poem, illustrated by Louise Brierley

CHAPTER 5

Hearing Voices

The Secret Song

Who saw the petals
drop from the rose?
I, said the spider.
But nobody knows.

Who saw the sunset
flash on a bird?
I, said the fish
But nobody heard.

Who saw the fog
come over the sea?
I, said the sea pigeon
Only me.

Who saw the first
green light of the sun?
I, said the night owl,
The only one.

Who saw the moss
creep over the stone?
I, said the grey fox,
All alone.

Margaret Wise Brown

Many of the poets writing for young people feature voices of all kinds. These "talking poems" can take different forms, for example:

- *monologues*, in which the voice and the unseen audience provide sources for role-playing by the children
- *dialogues*, which can serve as minimal scripts for the children to interpret in pairs, in small groups, or as a whole class divided into parts
- *question and answer poems*, where children can explore the voices of who may be speaking
- *chants, cheers, prayers, invocations, and songs*, where children can raise their voices together as a village, a tribe, a society, players in a game
- *situations so intense and concentrated* that role-playing and improvisation present ways of discovering the voices within the poems

Finding the voices in a poem can lead children to a careful examination of how the poem is structured. Because most poems are condensed and intense forms, the puzzlements that arise make for thoughtful discussion. Of course, narration can be an implied voice by the poet, or children can add characters to speak the words. Often, suggesting a setting or a context for a poem can add to the quality of the work. In "The Secret Song," students can represent the narrator as different characters that ask the questions. Will there be one or more characters? Who might they be? Mother Nature perhaps? And why are these questions being asked at this time? You and your students can explore how they might become participants in a poem by being in role and adding a sense of drama to the oral reading.

Talking About Poetry

To really understand a poem, it often helps to talk about it, to discuss ideas and feelings with others in your group. This plan may help you get started:

Divide into groups of four.

❏ In each group, determine who will jot down the ideas and opinions of group members. A report will be made later. (The job of recorder could rotate among group members.)

❏ Read the poem you have been given silently.

❏ Next, read the poem out loud taking turns and helping one another.

❏ On your own, take a mental walk through the poem, pausing at what interests you. You might notice the story, a new idea or a new way of expressing an old idea, images based on the senses, rhythm, rhyme or other sound structures, or personal feelings. Don't worry about being wrong—there are no right answers.

❏ When everyone in the group has completed the mental walk, the recorder will ask each person to contribute one thing he or she has noticed and write it down.

❏ Everyone must contribute something to the activity. You may take several turns.

❏ The goal of "poem talk" is to listen to the thoughts of the members of your group and to add to your own meaning making about the poem, the poet, and the different responses to the poetic experience by your classmates. You will find that you develop your ideas faster by "hitchhiking" on the contributions of others, modifying and extending our own impressions.

❏ When your group has finished recording, the teacher will call you back together and each group recorder will report.

❏ When you have listened to all the reports, your teacher might challenge the class to think about additional ideas. (Example: What makes this a poem rather than a description?) You will then gain more opportunities to talk about the poem or to ask questions.

Let's Have a Conversation

A Demonstration

Think about what it means when people are described as "making small talk." Is this easy for everyone to do?

> As Tommy Snooks and Bessy Brooks
> Were walking out one Sunday,
> Says Tommy Snooks to Bessy Brooks,
> "Tomorrow will be Monday."

- Children can discuss a question such as this: "Have you ever been in a situation where your thoughts dried up and you said things you felt embarrassed about later?" Together, they can create a list of typical small talk expressions that they hear every day, and order them in such a way that the effect is like a "found poem." In one Grade 6 classroom, oral improvisation with this old nursery rhyme led to a discussion of what people say in certain social situations and how they say it. Poor Tommy Snook's inability to carry on a proper conversation with the woman he was smitten by led to the creation of some "small talk" compositions that the students, working in small groups, performed out loud.

- First, the students brainstormed and jotted down typical small talk expressions. *Nice day! Terrible weather! How about those Raptors!* Next, they brainstormed examples of small talk expressions that were made up of words slurred together, such as "wazzup" and "whajasay." Finally, they listed any small talk expressions as words that had attitude, such as *Yo! Not! I don't think so!*

- Using the list pattern as a sound map, the students now selected and arranged a six to eight line piece drawn from their hoard of ideas. They were trying to create an interesting sound pattern. Repetition of parts could be included. Composing in this way necessitated that the students read their work aloud again and again as they edited, revised, and reordered. Here is a sample from one group. They used solos building to a crescendo when all voices came together on the last word.

Wazzup? Whajasay?
Wazzup? Whajasay?
Gonna rain. No way!
Got the time?
Gotta dime?
Gotta go
Split!

Discovering Voices

These poems have been selected for their voices—all kinds of voices. You can explore them together as a class, groups can all interpret one poem differently, or each group can work with a different poem. The point of this exploration is to awaken you to the voices heard (and sometimes hidden) inside poems, so that you can breathe life into the words.

The Pie

Who made the pie?
I did.
Who stole the pie?
He did.
Who found the pie?
She did.
Who ate the pie?
You did.
Who cried for pie?
We all did.

Me

Me me me me
No one else but me!
Me me my mine
No one else could shine so fine!
Number one all of the time.
Numero Uno! Yo! It's me
I'm the one I want to be,
My myself me and I
I'm no one else, don't want to try.

Rabbit and Lark

"Under the ground
    It's rumbly and dark
and interesting,"
    Said Rabbit to Lark.

Said Lark to Rabbit,
    "Up in the sky
There's plenty of room
    And it's airy and high."

"Under the ground
    It's warm and dry.
Won't you live with me?"
    Was Rabbit's reply.
"The air's so sunny.
    I wish you'd agree,"
Said the little Lark,
    "To live with me."

But under the ground
    And up in the sky,
Larks can't burrow
    Nor rabbits fly.

So Skylark over
    And Rabbit under
They had to settle
    To live asunder.

And often these two friends
    Meet with a will
For a chat together
    On top of the hill.

James Reeves

The Grasshopper and the Ants

The grasshopper fiddled
The whole summer long.
He filled the green fields
With his bright, silly song.

The ants, on the other hand,
Worked up a sweat,
Putting away
All the goods they could get.

When wintertime came,
The poor hopper was famished,
For all of his food
Had entirely vanished.

"Please feed me!" he begged,
"Or—alas—I will die."
"Go lunch on your fiddle,"
The ants did reply.

MORAL
Whether a star
Or a low second-rater,
Only play now
And you'll have to pay later.

Jane Yolen

The Storm

First there were two of us, then there were three of us,
Then there was one bird more,
Four of us—wild white sea-birds,
Treading the ocean floor;
And the *wind* rose, and the *sea* rose,
To the angry billows' roar—
With one of us—two of us—three of us—four of us
Sea-birds on the shore.

Soon there were five of us, soon there were nine of us,
And lo! in a trice sixteen!
And the yeasty surf curdled over the sands,
The gaunt grey rocks between;
And the tempest raved, and the lightning's fire
Struck blue on the spindrift hoar—
And on four of us—ay, and on four times four of us
Sea-birds on the shore.

And our sixteen waxed to thirty-two,
And they to past three score—
A wild, white welter of winnowing wings,
And ever more and more;
And the winds lulled, and the sea went down,
And the sun streamed out on high,
Gilding the pools and the spume and the spars
'Neath the vast blue deeps of the sky;

And the isles and the bright green headlands shone,
As they'd never shone before,
Mountains and valleys of silver cloud,
Wherein to swing, sweep, soar—
A host of screeching, scolding, scrabbling
Sea-birds on the shore—
A snowy, silent, sun-washed drift
Of sea-birds on the shore.

Walter de la Mare

- This poem asks for movement to accompany the words. The sea-birds can enter the circle, first two, then three, and so on, until everyone is part of the flock on the shore. The lines can be divided up and spoken by the sea-birds.

Asking Questions

The man in the wilderness asked of me,
How many strawberries grew in the sea?
I answered him, as I thought good,
As many red herrings as grew in the wood.

Characters in poems from the oral tradition often ask tough questions. In many instances, finding the answers to the questions leads to an exciting adventure.

In the poem below, the celebrated author Russell Hoban uses the question-and-answer form and the rhythms of the oral tradition to create the sense of the ocean.

Old Man Ocean, how do you pound
Smooth glass rough, rough stones round?
Time and the tide and the wild waves rolling,
Night and the wind and the long grey dawn.

Old Man Ocean, what do you tell,
What do you sing in the empty shell?
Fog and the storm and the long bell tolling,
Bones in the deep and the brave men gone.

Here, questions raised by a student named Jonathan build suspense as the reader begins to imagine the answers.

What's that down there?
What's that moving?
What's that moving down
in the dark?
Is it the monster
Who roars
And kills?
Or is it the skeleton
Who rattles his bones?

What's that down there?
What's that moving?
What's that moving down
in the dark?
Is it a bat?
Flying through the air?
What's that
in the dark?

- You can write a question or a question-and-answer poem like Jonathan.
- What questions can you brainstorm as a class to write a poem about? (One class posts a list of questions to use when students need a beginning place.)
- Could one classmate ask you a question to form the basis of your poem, while you ask that person a question to write about? Find out.

Remembering Street Cries

A Demonstration

For a century, the cry "Young lambs to sell" brought children running into the street with their pennies and halfpennies. The toy lambs had white cotton wool fleeces spangled with Dutch gilt, heads of flour paste, horns and legs of tin, and collars of pink tape.

> Young lambs to sell! Young lambs to sell!
> If I'd as much money as I could tell,
> I'd not come here with lambs to sell!
> Dolly and Molly, Richard and Nell,
> Buy my young lambs and I'll use you well!

The nursery rhyme,

> Tom Tom the Piper's son
> Stole a pig and away he run,

often arouses children's concern about the stolen pig being eaten. In *The Oxford Dictionary of Nursery Rhymes*, Iona and Peter Opie say that modern illustrators depict the scene incorrectly. "The pig was not a live one but a sweetmeat model sold by a street hawker, as is narrated in the chapbooks. 'This man makes pigs of paste and fills their bellies with currants and places two little currants in their heads for eyes.' Vendors of such pigs were common in the eighteenth century."

- Discuss with the class whether any "street criers" are left. What examples can the students come up with? They might interview senior citizens about street criers they may remember.
- Students could pool their findings for an oral performance, a soundscape that might have been heard in their community a hundred years ago. Discuss how these cries could be brought to life. The students could re-create a market where the voices are heard all at once, then gradually fade out until the market closes.
- Another option is for students to make contemporary street cries from ads for products and services in their community.
- The street cries featured on the next page can be the basis for individual monologues or choral speaking. Students can work in pairs finding ways to turn the words into street cries. (The one by Walter de la Mare requires a narrator: Who will that be?)
- If possible, have the students try out their street cries on the playground or in a stairwell where they can raise their voices as a market would sound—first, one voice, then two voices, and so on.

Street Cries

Get ready your money and come to me,
I sell a young lamb for one penny
Young lambs to sell! Young lambs to sell!
If I'd as much money as I could tell,
I never would cry, Young lambs to sell!

Here's Finiky Hawkes,
As busy as any;
Will well black your shoes,
And charge but a penny.

If I'd as much money as I could spend,
I never would cry, Old chairs to mend.
Old chairs to mend! Old chairs to mend!
I never would cry, Old chairs to mend.

Here I am with my rabbits
Hanging on my pole,
The finest Hampshire rabbits
That e'er crept from a hole.

"Cherries, ripe cherries!"
The old woman cried,
In her snowy white apron,
And basket beside;
And the little boys came,
Eyes shining, cheeks red,
To buy bags of cherries,
To eat with their bread.

Walter de la Mare

Here's a large one for the lady,
Here's a small one for the baby;
Come buy, my pretty lady,
Come buy o'me a broom.

Young gentlemen attend my cry,
    And bring forth all your Knives;
The barbers Razors too I grind;
    Bring out your scissors, wives.

Who wants some pudding nice and hot!
    'Tis now the time to try it;
Just taken from the smoking pot,
    And taste before you buy it.

When Words Sing

We often forget the poetry of much of the music both past and present. Lyrics are integral to the songs of teenagers today, and many of them download and buy them with each CD. Rhymes that are also songs can be spoken and then sung. You might use the traditional verses below to let students explore how mood shifts dramatically depending on whether words are spoken or sung.

Can you make me a cambric shirt,
  Parsley, sage, rosemary, and thyme,
Without any seam or needlework?
  And you shall be a true lover of mine.

Can you wash it in yonder well,
  Parsley, sage, rosemary, and thyme,
Where never sprung water, nor rain ever fell
  And you shall be a true lover of mine.

Can you dry it on yonder thorn,
  Parsley, sage, rosemary, and thyme,
Which never bore blossom since Adam was born
  And you shall be a true lover of mine.

Now you've asked me questions three,
  Parsley, sage, rosemary, and thyme,
I hope you'll answer as many for me,
  And you shall be a true lover of mine.

Can you find me an acre of land,
  Parsley, sage, rosemary, and thyme.
Between the salt water and the sea sand?
  And you shall be a true lover of mine.

Can you plough it with a ram's horn,
  Parsley, sage, rosemary, and thyme,
And sow it all over with one peppercorn?
  And you shall be a true lover of mine.

Can you reap it with a sickle of leather,
  Parsley, sage, rosemary, and thyme,
And bind it up with a peacock's feather?
  And you shall be a true lover of mine.

When you have done and finished your work
  Parsley, sage, rosemary, and thyme,
Then come to me for your cambric shirt,
  And you shall be a true lover of mine.

Performing Story Poems

For years we have enjoyed working with children and adults to bring the words of poets to life in performances. Experiences have ranged from groups sharing their interpretations with the other members of the class to parents' evenings where the entire show was created from poetry.

James Reaney is a poet and a playwright who writes about life in his hometown. In this excerpt from the play *Names and Nicknames*, he celebrates the school as the heart of the community. The joy comes from the blending of the words into a memory piece of childhood that existed there and then.

James Reaney was interested in using the sounds of "memory" words to paint a picture of a particular time and in the readers' need to explore the many ways that a word, a phrase, or a line could be spoken so that everything adds to the picture being re-created. The story in our minds is created by the memories evoked by the words.

You can experiment with a variety of ways of bringing these verses to life. James Reaney would, no doubt, enjoy all of their versions.

- The selection is rich in sound possibilities. As you read it aloud, the children can make mental notes of where sound effects, singing, chanting, body sounds (clapping, snapping, snapping, stamping, and so on), solo voices, and chorus voices might be used.
- The class can look at the piece again and find opportunities where movement or ritual (e.g., circle or line games) might be used.
- Together, the children can divide the selection into four sections, and then divide into four groups.
- Groups can explore different ways of bringing the words in their sections to life. Each group prepares by reading silently, reading out loud in unison, and reading with solo and chorus voices.
- Groups can then experiment with sound effects, adding them where appropriate.
- Next, they can incorporate "frozen pictures" or movement that would enhance the piece.
- When all groups have finished preparing, they can come together as a class to share their work and create a complete version of the poem.

Excerpt from *Names and Nicknames*

Spring on Farmer Dell's Farm.
The snow has melted, the snow has gone
Tra la la   Tra la la   Tra la la
The bare trees have put their green leaves on
Tra la la   Tra la la   Tra la la
Knee deep knee deep knee deep knee deep
The frogs in the pond sing
Knee deep knee deep knee deep knee deep
The frogs in the pond sing

A schoolyard A schoolyard A schoolyard
Where is the schoolyard
Where the ground is stamped hard
With the children's stamping feet
We're on the way to find it
Find it find it
On the way to school
Dew dist mud hail
Snow ice frost smoke
Road lane ditch track
Truant officer
Tree
Pebble
Water
Splash!

In the School Room
Desk bell map chart
Clock book slate globe
Chalk paper ferrule ouch!
Blackboard children teacher printer
Student satchel pencil crayon
Register ink-bottle dictionary

What pupils do
Read write parse solve
Think reckon think learn
Think listen think attend
Study recite declaim—
Recollect and reckon compose compute
Recollect recollect recollect—
Remembrance remember remembrance
Calculate analyze

Recess recess! Games! games!
A schoolyard A schoolyard A schoolyard
Where the ground is hard
With the stamping children's feet

They stamp their feet, then break into a games sequence.

Crack the whip!
Send them flying!
Prisoner's base

Have kids on stilts, playing tug of war, etc.

Skipping skipping. The girls are skipping
Rosy apple lemon pear
These are the colours she should wear
The boys are walking on stilts
I am a girl guide dressed in blue
Skipping skipping. The girls are skipping.

A child who is "it" counts up to ten and then yells—

Anybody hiding round my goal
Whether he be hidden or not
He shall be caught
One two three on Walter!

A schoolyard A schoolyard A schoolyard
Where is the schoolyard
Where the ground is stamped hard
With the children's stamping feet
We're on the way to find it

James Reaney

Interpreting "Ten Tall Oaktrees"

"Ten Tall Oaktrees" is a dramatic story poem that you can bring to life. Students can read it aloud with solos, choruses, and sound effects.

Ten Tall Oaktrees

Ten tall oaktrees,
Standing in a line,
"Warships," cried King Henry,
Then there were nine.

Nine tall oaktrees,
Growing strong and straight,
"Charcoal," breathed the furnace,
Then there were eight.

Eight tall oaktrees,
Reaching towards heaven,
"Sizzle," spoke the lightning,
Then there were seven.

Seven tall oaktrees,
Branches, leaves and sticks,
"Firewood," smiled the merchant,
Then there were six.

Six tall oaktrees,
Glad to be alive,
"Barrels," boomed the brewery,
Then there were five.

Five tall oaktrees,
Suddenly a roar,
"Gangway," screamed the west wind,
Then there were four.

Four tall oaktrees,
Sighing like the sea,
"Floorboards," beamed the builder,
Then there were three.

Three tall oaktrees,
Groaning as trees do,
"Unsafe," claimed the council,
Then there were two.

Two tall oaktrees,
Spreading in the sun,
"Progress," snarled the by-pass,
Then there was one.

One tall oaktree,
Wishing it could run,
"Nuisance," grumped the farmer,
Then there were none.

No tall oaktrees,
Search the fields in vain:
Only empty skylines
And the cold, grey rain.

Richard Edwards

Michael Rosen's Characters

Michael Rosen was born in Harrow, England, and grew up in a home that was filled with books and with talk about literature. He attended medical school, then changed his mind about becoming a doctor. Instead, he read English Literature at Oxford University. When he began to write poetry, he wrote of his own childhood in the language of childhood. Writing from the child's point of view was not something that had been done widely and at first he had difficulty getting published. However, he became wildly popular both as a writer and as a broadcaster for the BBC (British Broadcasting Corporation). Since his first book, *Mind Your Own Business*, Michael has published poetry anthologies, short stories, picture book poetry, and books for secondary students and teachers on writing poetry.

I'm the youngest in our house
so it goes like this:

My brother comes in and says:
"Tell him to clear the fluff
out from under his bed."
Mum says,
"Clear the fluff
out from under your bed."
Father says,
"You heard what your mother said."
"What?" I say.
"The fluff," he says.
"Clear the fluff
out from under your bed."
So I say,
"There's fluff under his bed, too,
you know."

So father says,
"But we're talking about the fluff
under your bed."
"You will clear it up
won't you?" mum says.
So now my brother—all puffed up—
says,
"Clear the fluff
out from under your bed,
clear the fluff
out from under your bed."
Now I'm angry. I am angry.
So I say—what shall I say'?
I say,
"Shuttup stinks
YOU CAN'T RULE MY LIFE."

We're Going on a Bear Hunt, illustrated by Helen Oxenbury
A World of Poetry
You Can't Catch Me!, illustrated by Quentin Blake
Quick, Let's Get out of Here, illustrated by Quentin Blake
Under the Bed, illustrated by Quentin Blake
Smelly Jelly Smellyfish: The Seaside Book, illustrated by Quentin Blake
Centrally Heated Knickers, illustrated by Harry Horse
Rover, illustrated by Neal Layton
Even More Nonsense from Michael Rosen, illustrated by Clare Mackie
You Tell Me (with Roger McGough)
You Wait Till I'm Older Than You!, illustrated by Shoo Rayner

CHAPTER 6

Uncovering the Stories

My Hard Repair Job

In the awful quarrel
we had, my temper burnt
our friendship to cinders.
How can I make it whole
  again?

This way, that way,
that time, this time,
I pick up the burnt bits,
trying to change them back.

James Berry

Finding and reconstructing the stories hidden within poems offers a powerful dynamic for learning. Children can use story talk as the starting point for projects of all kinds—research, role-playing, writing, storytelling, reading aloud, painting. By beginning with talk, the teacher allows all the areas of concern to the children to be brought into the open. Children can begin making meaning, both personal and collective, using the medium of talk—invisible print that can be edited and reformed so easily —to understand the depth of the poems.

So many poems merely hint at stories, haunting our imaginations. Although many poems can be read right through for their stories, others demand a slower, closer reading, and only when we give free rein to our curiosity and imagination does the bigger story begin to emerge. Such is the case with "The Titanic."

The Titanic

Under the ocean where water falls
over the decks and tilted walls
where the sea comes knocking at the great ship's door,
the band still plays
to the drum of the waves,
to the drum of the waves.

Down in the indigo depths of the sea
the white shark waltzes gracefully
down the water-stairway, across the ballroom floor
where the cold shoals flow,
and ghost dancers go,
ghost dancers go.

Their dresses are frayed, their shoes are lost,
their jewels and beads and bones are tossed
into the sand, all turned to stone,
as they sing in the sea
eternally,
eternally.

Currents comb their long loose hair,
dancers sway forever where
the bright fish nibble their glittering bones,
till they fall asleep
in the shivering deep,
in the shivering deep.

Gillian Clark

Inside and Outside the Poem

A Demonstration

I heard a horseman
    Ride over the hill;
The moon shone clear,
    The night was still;

His helm was silver,
    And pale was he;
And the horse he rode
    Was of ivory.

Walter de la Mare

Poetry contains some of the best moon lore. Whether the moon is being jumped over, used as a clothes dryer, or escaped to, stories abound.

"Flying-man, flying-man,
Up in the sky,
Where are you going to,
Flying so high?"

"Over the mountains,
And over the sea."
"Flying-man, Flying-man,
Can't you take me."

Short verses, such as "Flying-Man," can generate much discussion. The points below emerged in a talk with Shahlena and Casey, nine-year-olds who had read "Flying-Man."

It might be Superman or a bird, a man with magic powers, a man with wings, a man wearing a cape, a good guy, but maybe not.

He is flying so high that he can't hit mountains. Perhaps he is trying to get away from something like the police or prison, or maybe he is going on holidays.

I think that a person is thinking this poem, but Flying-Man can't hear it. It sounds like they're sitting and thinking about Flying-Man.

Maybe they're sitting on a mountain or in a forest or on a boat. They can climb on the mast of a boat to see the Flying-Man.

- "Flying-Man" gives no clues about how the individual flies. Perhaps the students could design some flying machines or devices that might do the job.
- Students might create a themed anthology of moon verse selected from various poetry collections. They could accompany the verses with drawings that try to capture the many facets of "moon people" presented.

Role Playing with the Poem

Hark, hark, the dogs do bark,
The beggars are coming to town;
Some in jags, and some in rags,
And some in velvet gowns.

Some gave them white bread,
And some gave them brown,
And some gave them a good horse-whip,
And sent them out of town.

Often, as in the selection above, poems provide few details, but suggest much. To find more in the rhyme, it is best to work with the story, fleshing it out and adding to it.

- Form groups of four and list the possible storytellers who are saying the words. For example, could it be the voice of the local police constables or worried merchants?
- The incident is briefly described, but we don't know a lot about it. In your group of four, brainstorm all the questions that remain unanswered. For example, should we be afraid of the beggars?
- In each group, have one person take the role of the mayor. The others are citizens of the town. Prepare a one-minute scene which explains how the townspeople feel about the invasion of beggars. Your scene should have a definite beginning (what you are doing before the beggars show up), middle (how you react to the presence of the beggars) and an ending (what you, as townspeople, do about it).
- Write personal memories of the day long ago when the beggar horde converged on the writer's town. Write them as a list poem *or* write a letter to a relative in another place describing what happened when the beggars came to your town.

O I have been to the meadow-bout fields,
And I have been to the gorses;
And I have been to the meadow-bout fields,
To seek my master's horses.
And I got wet, and very very wet,
And I got wet and weary,
And I was wet, and very very wet
When I came home to Mary!

This story gives only a few clues to the bigger story around it.

- Work with a partner and make a list of questions you would like the speaker of the poem to answer.
- One partner takes the role of the speaker; the other takes the role of the master whose horses are lost. Improvise the interview that might take place between the pair.
- Some groups may want to share their interpretations.

Talking About Stories

A Demonstration

Constructing the stories hidden within poems offers a powerful dynamic for learning. The discussion can be spontaneous or directed by the teacher, and the children can put forward their own concerns. They can use story talk as the starting point for projects of all kinds—research, role-playing, writing, storytelling, reading aloud, and painting. By beginning with talk, the teacher allows all the areas of concern to the children to be brought into the open, so that they can begin making meaning, both personal and collective, using the medium of talk—invisible print that can be edited and reformed so easily—to understand the depth of the poems.

Talk with the whole class is effective, but presents some difficulties. The number of children who can respond during the session is limited by time, opportunity, the ability of each child to speak aloud in large groups, and the group's ability to listen and respond sensitively and meaningfully. As well, it may be difficult to hear everyone unless the furniture is rearranged. However, talk with the whole class presents a public forum for shared common experiences related to the poems. It can allow for reflective talk after other response modes have been explored. Children can talk about the pictorial representations, the writing, the drama, the research, and so on. The talk may focus on the meanings or on the storyteller, on the children's identification with the story, on the stories within the poem, on the background information, on the conflict, the resolution, the use of language, the difficulty of idiom, the word choice, the sentence structure, or the style. It is important that the talk, at times, be focused on the poem itself, whether at the beginning or as a summary or reflection of the dialogue that has taken place. The children may leave the poem in order to understand it better, but they should return to see its reflection in the new learning, the new meaning that has grown from the talk.

Bessy Bell and Mary Gray
   They were two bonnie lassies:
They built their house upon the lea
   And covered it with rushes.

Bessy kept the garden gate,
   And Mary kept the pantry;
Bessy always had to wait,
   While Mary lived in plenty.

This nursery rhyme raises many questions for discusssion:

- Why did two attractive young women (bonnie lassies) choose to take up residence in a remote area (upon the lea)?
- Why were they living in such makeshift circumstances (covered it with rushes)?
- What was their relationship? Were they friends? cousins? coworkers?
- Why was a well-to-do person living this way (Mary lived in plenty)?
- Did Bessie have any choice in this matter (Bessie had to wait)?
- Were the two women fleeing from difficult circumstances (love affair gone awry; natural disaster; war; escape from someone)?
- Does the story have a happy ending?

The story of Bessy Bell and Mary Gray may be a true story and the nursery rhyme an elliptical version of an old Scottish ballad. It appears that the two women were indeed friends, and it was while Bessy was visiting Mary (about 1645) that the plague broke out in Perth, seven miles away from Mary's village. In order to escape it, the two women fled to what they hoped was safer ground. Eventually, they caught the plague from the young man who brought them their provisions and who was also in love with them, and they died. Approximately 3,000 people are thought to have fallen to the plague in that region and it is likely that the two women were already infected when they fled.

Retelling the Stories in Poems

A Demonstration

Spontaneous retelling in a circle is one of the most effective ways in which students can reveal what a story rhyme they have just heard has meant to them. With such retelling, no one has the burden of the entire story rhyme.

- As the story travels around the circle, each participant can add as much or as little as desired.
- Some students prefer to pass on the initial round or so until they begin to get more involved in the story.
- The beauty of this activity is its simplicity and the opportunity it affords students to put the story rhyme into their own words and to make explicit personal story imagery.
- In the context of a new rhyme, we often ask the students, in a circle, how they feel and think about the characters.
- We then may come out of the circle and conduct interviews with one another. "Let's interview this person. Pretend you are a reporter. What would you like to ask? What would you like to know?" That simple technique gets the students talking about the characters.
- Next, we might have the whole group together, telling stories at once; alternatively, we might have a surprise interview with a character, at which only three key questions, just like the three wishes so common in folktales, can be asked.
- We then help the students to refine their understanding of what they think is important about the story rhyme, discussing and struggling with the three questions.
- The storytelling circle shares the telling of the story rhyme on more time, this time revealing a secret discovered about it.

You might work with this poem for storytelling.

Mr. Finney's Turnip

Mr. Finney had a turnip
   And it grew behind the barn;
And it grew and it grew,
   And that turnip did no harm.

There it grew and it grew
   Till it could grow no longer;
Then his daughter Lizzie picked it
   And put it in the cellar.

There it lay and it lay
   Till it began to rot;
And his daughter Suzie took it
   And put it in the pot.

And they boiled it and boiled it
   As long as they were able;
And then his daughters took it
   And put it on the table.

Mr. Finney and his wife
   They sat them down to sup;
And they ate and they ate
   And they ate that turnip up.

A Novel Approach to Poetry

A Demonstration

Several authors for young people have found that the poetical voice offers them an evocative and intriguing format for structuring their novels, and we are fortunate to have these transformations of genres for our students to experience. These poem-narratives promote a variety of responses as the style and story mix and mingle and reveal an aesthetic appeal that draws the reader into both the narrative and the shape of the words. Often written as monologues, the pages offer students opportunities for reading them aloud, for grouping several excerpts together into a dramatized sharing, or for adding the unspoken lines of those characters mentioned in the telling.

- Karen Hesse won the Newbery medal for her novel *Out of the Dust*. She used free-verse poems to tell the story of life during the dust storms of the 1930s. The spare text demonstrates the poetry of everyday language and fills the pages with memorable images of hope in the midst of despair. Then, in *Witness*, Karen Hesse writes a novel in the same clear, free verse, encompassing the voices of 11 townspeople in Vermont who are involved in the activities of the Ku Klux Klan in the 1920s. In this lyrical and powerful novel created through poetry, history is brought to life through these glimpses of small town life. Her new novel, *Aleutian Sparrow*, takes place in 1942 on the Aleutian Islands.

- Cynthia Rylant's book of poems, *Waiting to Waltz*, is autobiographical. It was inspired by her experiences growing up in the little town of Beaver, West Virginia, where she lived between the ages of 8 and 18. As you read the selections, the town becomes real in front of your eyes, and you end by caring about everyone who is given a poetical voice. In *Something Permanent*, Cynthia Rylant was inspired to write poems to accompany the photographs of Walker Evans who took photographs of the poor after the Depression. The blending of the two art forms creates a moving story about this sad time in the lives of so many.

- The award-winning poet Marilyn Nelson provides a detailed portrait of George Washington Carver, who rose from slavery to become a leader for the landless black farmers, as well as a noted botanist and inventor. The voices of the people drawn in her poems create the life of not only Carver but of his works in the southern United States.

- Newbery award winner Sharon Creech uses poetry in a fascinating way in *Love That Dog*. Her main character, Jack, is in Miss Stretchberry's fifth-grade class. He hates poetry. How this teacher leads Jack into a world of meaningful poems through connecting with an actual author (Walter Dean Myers) offers us a plan for engaging our own students in this word wonder.

- Kevin Major, in *Ann and Seamus*, provides a poetic retelling of how lives were saved during the wreck of an Irish immigrant ship off Newfoundland in 1928.

- In *Shakespeare Bats Cleanup*, Ron Coertge writes a funny and poignant novel in free verse about 14-year-old Kevin Boland, diagnosed with "mono," who finds poetry amid his baseball dreams.

Naomi Shihab Nye's Eyes

Naomi Shihab Nye was born in St. Louis, Missouri, to a Palestinian father and an American mother. She attended Trinity University in San Antonio, Texas, where she still lives with her family. She has twice travelled to the Middle East and Asia for the United States Information Agency promoting international goodwill through the arts.

"To me the world of poetry is a house with thousands of glittering windows," say Naomi Shihab Nye. "Our words and images, land to land, era to era, shed light on one another. Our words dissolve the shadows we imagine fall between. 'One night I dreamt of spring,' writes Syrian poet Muhammad al-Maghut, 'and when I awoke, flowers covered my pillow.' Isn't this where empathy begins? Other countries stop seeming quite so 'foreign,' or inanimate, or strange, when we listen to the intimate voices of their citizens. If poetry comes out of the deepest places in the human soul and experience, shouldn't it be as important to learn about one another's poetry, country to country, as one another's weather or gross national products? It seems critical to me."

Welcome to Abu Dhabi,
the Minister of Culture said.
You may hold my falcon as we visit.
He slipped a leather band around my arm
and urged the bird to step on board.
It wore a shapely leather hood.
Or otherwise, the host described,
the bird might pluck your very eyes.
My very eyes were blinking hard
behind the glasses that they wore.
The falcon's claws, so hooked and huge,
gripped firmly on the leather band.
I had to hold my arm out high.

My hand went numb. The heavens shone
a giant gold beyond our room.
I had no memory why I'd come
to see this man.
A falcon dives, and rips, and kills!
I think he likes you though.
It was the most I could have hoped for then.
We mentioned art.
We drank some tea.
He offered to remove the hood.
I said the bird looked very good just wearing it.
All right by me.

Naomi Shihab Nye

---

19 Varieties of Gazelle: Poems of the Middle East

What Have You Lost?

Fuel: Poems

Words Under the Words: Selected Poems

I Feel a Little Jumpy Around You: A Book of Her Poems & His Poems Collected in Pairs

The Tree Is Older Than You Are: A Bilingual Gathering of Poems & Stories from Mexico with Paintings by Mexican Artists

Come with Me: Poems for a Journey, illustrated by Dan Yaccarino

This Same Sky: A Collection of Poems from Around the World

Salting the Ocean: 100 Poems by Young Poets

CHAPTER 7

Exploring Games and Ceremonies

Old Man Wind,
Why do you blow the trees to
  make them shiver?
Why do you whistle in the
  small gaps?
Why do you roar like a
  hundred dragons?
Why do you chase the gentle
  leaves?
Why do you push the small
  green grass?
Why do you pull my hair?
Go away
Until I want you
To fly my kite.

Mark

Poems have been important parts of ceremonies and rituals for centuries. Some of them can be dramatized as rituals and ceremonies that the children invent. This poem by Robert Fisher is based on a Greek myth.

Minotaur

in the middle of the sea lies an island
in the middle of the island stands a palace
in the middle of the palace is a maze
of darkened rooms and alleyways
endless walls and hidden doors
miles and miles of corridors
here shadows fall and footsteps sound
echoing along the ground
here is my home
I am minotaur
half-man half-bull
shaggy-headed golden horns
hear me bellow hear my roar
see the slavering of my jaw
round the corner here I wait
flaring nostrils sniff the air
for here or somewhere a door may open
and I will enter
your dream
of the sea
and in the middle of the sea lies an island
in the middle of the island stands a palace
in the middle of the palace is a maze
of darkened rooms and alleyways
endless walls and hidden doors
miles and miles of corridors
here shadows fall and footsteps sound
echoing along the ground
here is my home
I am ... waiting

- The poem can be read aloud in variety of ways. For example, the minotaur's voice can echo from the walls of a cave, as students, one by one, join in the reading, echoing the last word at the end of a line.
- The students could take the roles of archeologists, attempting to read the words etched into the walls of a cave.
- If this poem is presented with participants standing in a circle, it can be turned into a ceremony where people are remembering the minotaur story as a warning.

Family Rituals

Bingo

Saturday night
Dad washed, I dried
the supper dishes
while Mom armed herself
for Early Bird bingo at seven
in the church basement:
Her lucky piece
(a smooth quarter she'd won the first time
    out),
seat cushion,
and a white Owl's box of pink plastic markers.

Dad read the paper
watched TV with me
until Mom returned,
announcing her triumph with a door slam
and a shout
"I was hot!"

Flinging her hat,
twirling out of her jacket,
she pulled dollar bills
from her pockets
before setting them free
to flutter like fat spring snow.

"Ninety-two dollars!" she squealed
as Dad hugged her off the floor.
"Ninety-two dollars!"

In bed I listened to
mumbled voices
planning to spend the money—
on groceries
school clothes
a leaky radiator—
and wished she'd buy
a shiny red dress
long white gloves
and clickety-click high heels.

Paul Janeczko

The poem "Bingo" describes a family ritual. Sometimes, such little rituals and ceremonies are so familiar to us that we don't notice how significant they are in our lives until they disappear. Then we realize that something is missing.

- You can develop a poem from a family or neighborhood event. You might write it as if the event is to be taken very seriously. Consider these occasions: a holiday dinner, a religious occasion, a backyard barbeque, a sleepover, a Friday evening, a sports event, a grocery shopping ritual.
- You might want to add movement or music to dramatize the ritual you describe.

From Games into Poetry

A Demonstration

For younger children, the charms of games, counting-out rhymes, rituals, and chants probably lie in the simple words and the mesmerizing repetition. Later, the appeal will be in the tricks of language that the rhymes offer.

> Children today play games that are known in tribal Africa and were familiar in ancient Rome. When a child climbs a pile of stones and shouts "I'm the king of the castle, get down you dirty rascal!" he is repeating a Roman citizen's taunt; when an older boy or girl shows a baby the "two little birds sitting on a hill, one named Jack and the other named Jill," she or he is rehearsing a nursery entertainment known on four continents.
>
> *Alison Lurie*

Just as children's oral traditions—games, rhymes, riddles, jokes—have connections in history, archaeology, anthropology, literature, popular culture, and art, so too do many poems.

Some nursery rhymes are complete dramas that children can enact. "Old Roger Is Dead and Laid in His Grave" is one example that we have seen played.

> Old Roger is dead and laid in his grave,
> Laid in his grave, laid in his grave;
> Old Roger is dead and laid in his grave,
> H'm ha! laid in his grave.

Children join hands in a circle and revolve around a child (Old Roger), covered by sweaters and coats, who lies in the centre of the circle.

> They planted an apple tree over his head,
> Over his head, over his head;
> They planted an apple tree over his head,
> H'm ha! over his head.

Children, still holding hands, advance towards Old Roger and lift their arms over their heads, as close to the body as possible, then retreat.

> The apples grew ripe and ready to fall,
> Ready to fall, ready to fall;
> The apples grew ripe and ready to fall
> H'm ha! ready to fall.

Children circle Old Roger in opposite directions, still linked.

> There came an old woman a-picking them all,
> A picking them all, a-picking them all;
> There came an old woman a-picking them all,
> H'm ha! picking them all.

Children drop hands and mime collecting apples.

> Old Roger jumps up and gives her a knock,
> Gives her a knock, gives her a knock;
> Which makes the old woman go hippety-hop
> H'm ha! hippety-hop.

Children continue apple picking, but must from time to time go as close to Old Roger as possible. At some point, Old Roger leaps out and chases the players. The one tagged now becomes Old Roger.

In this medieval French carol, the players form a line facing the leader and proceed in a call and response fashion.

All: Fal de ral la, Fal de ral la (*everyone take two steps to the right*)
          Hinkumdooby round about (*everyone turn in a circle*)
          Fal de ral la, Fal de ral la (*take two steps to the left*)
          Hinkumdooby round about (*everyone turn in a circle*)
Leader: Right hand in
All: Right hand in
Leader: Right hand out
All: Right hand out
All: Hinkumdooby round about (*clapping*)
All: Fal de ral la, Fal de ral la (*everyone take two steps to the right*)
          Hinkumdooby round about (*everyone turn in a circle*)
          Fal de ral la, Fal de ral la (*take two steps to the left*)
          Hinkumdooby round about (*everyone turn in a circle*)
Leader: Left hand in
All: Left hand in
Leader: Left hand out
All: Left hand out
All: Hinkumdooby round about (*clapping*)
          (*repeat chorus as before*)
Leader and group: Heads in, Heads out
                     Heads in, Heads out
                     (*repeat chorus*)
Leader and group: All in
                     All out
                     (*repeat chorus*)
Leader and group: All down
                     Bottoms on the floor
                     Hinkumdooby round about.
                     (*repeat several times getting softer and softer*)

Chanting Together

A Musical Beat

A chant is a poem meant to be read aloud. One or more lines are repeated over and over, creating a powerful rhythm that draws everyone into the language action, just as some rock and rap songs do. Chants may repeat or combine lines or phrases. They generally have a lilt or beat that seems musical.

Lillian Morrison talks about the history and purpose of chants in this way:

> The chant is one of the earliest forms of poetry, dating all the way back to the swirling mists of prehistoric time when cavepeople, sitting around smoking fires, made up magical spells and incantations to protect themselves from wild animals, hurricanes and fires, and to help themselves do well in the hunt, find good-looking mates, and have lots of healthy children. Blues songs, slave songs, and prison work songs all draw on the ancient form of the chant.

- The poem "Subway" can become a chant as everyone reads it together.

Subway

Here come tiger down the track
ROAW-O
Big white eye and a mile-long back
ROAW-O
Through the darkest cave he run
ROAW-O
Never see the sky or sun
ROAW-O

- By patterning this poem, you can create a chant about another modern invention. Come up with a metaphor to describe the invention's actions and then choose a "sound word" to add to the poem. You might want to choose one of these inventions: a washer and dryer, an excavating machine, a coal mine, a ferris wheel, a jetliner, an elevator or an escalator.

A New Creation

Explore the poem "Cat Began," as a dramatic chant.

Cat Began

CAT began.
She took the howling of the wind,
She took the screeching of the owl
And made her voice.

For her coat
She took the softness of the snow,
She took the yellow of the sand,
She took the shadows of the branches of the trees.

From deep wells
She took the silences of stones,
She took the moving of the water
For her walk.

Then at night
Cat took the glittering of stars,
She took the blackness of the sky
To make her eyes.

Fire and ice
Went in the sharpness of her claws
And for their shape
She took the new moon's slender curve—

And Cat was made.

Andrew Matthews

- How will the lines be spoken?
- Who will say the lines?
- Will there be movement as you speak?
- Who are the members of the chanting group—the cat people who remember this birth at special times of the year? the voices of those who watched?
- See if you can create a similar ceremony for "Dog Began."

DOG began.
He took the thunder from the mountain, . . .

Joseph Bruchac's World

Joseph Bruchac lives with his wife, Carol, in the Adirondack foothills town of Greenfield Center, New York, in the same house where his maternal grandparents raised him. Much of his writing draws on that land and his Abenaki ancestry. Although his American Indian heritage is only one part of an ethnic background that includes Slovak and English blood, he has been most nourished by those Native roots.

Bruchac holds a B.A. from Cornell University, an M.A. in Literature and Creative Writing from Syracuse, and a Ph.D. in Comparative Literature from the Union Institute of Ohio. His work as an educator includes eight years of directing a college program for Skidmore College inside a maximum security prison.

Bruchac has edited several highly praised anthologies of contemporary poetry and fiction. As a professional teller of the traditional tales of the Adirondacks and the Native peoples of the Northeastern Woodlands, he has performed widely in Europe and throughout the United States from Florida to Hawaii. He has been featured at such events as the British Storytelling Festival and the National Storytelling Festival in Jonesboro, Tennessee.

Longhouse Song

Elm bark is my skin
bent saplings my bones
my mouth that draws
in the living wind
is the door to the coming of sun.

My breath
is the smoke
rising up to join sky.
My heart is the fire
in the circle of stones.

My eyes, my spirit
and my thoughts
belong to those
who keep close to the earth
their dreams held
by the circle of seasons.

Joseph Bruchac

---

13 Moons on Turtle's Back (with J. London)
Between Earth and Sky
Keepers of the Earth (with M. Caduto)
Keepers of the Night (with M. Caduto)
Many Nations: An Alphabet of Native America
Seasons of the Circle
The Earth Under Sky Bear's Feet
The Wind Eagle

CHAPTER 8

Responding Through Poetry

Four a.m. in the Woods

Darkness softens, a thin
tissue of mist between trees.
One by one the day's
uncountable voices come out
like twilight fireflies, like stars.

The perceiving self sits
with his back against rough
 bark,
casting ten thousand questions
 into the future.
As shadows take shape, the
 curtains part
for the length of time it takes
 to gasp,
and behold, the purpose of his
life dawns on him.

Marilyn Nelson

Award-winning poet Marilyn Nelson found inspiration in the life of George Washington Carver. In her collection of poems named after the black inventor, botanist, teacher, artist, musician, and former slave, she provides a compelling and revealing portrait. The poem "Four a.m. in the Woods" is one entry from her book.

Students write throughout the day in school. If we take note of opportunities for composing poems as a normal activity in a variety of curriculum areas, we can help students to both represent their ideas and knowledge, and to add their own affective responses through poems. Poetic writing becomes a suitable strategy necessary when working with a variety of genres and information.

Genres, formats, and shapes offer us supportive structures for writing down our thoughts and feelings. We hitchhike along with the writers and artists who have motivated us into action, taking off from their initial creations, but making the work our own. We can transform a selection of print into another mode, taking the essence of the text and reworking it into another form, such as an excerpt from a novel as a poem. Transforming often means shifting the point of view, and may lead to a deeper understanding of the text that is being patterned.

Poems can grow from a topic or an issue drawn from the students' own interests and questions that stimulate their curiosity and cause them to want to find answers or solutions. Poetry can grow from science or social studies as well, or from the themes in novels and picture books.

Ideas for Poems

- One of the simplest things for students to write is a poem in the form of a letter. Today we have books of letters, written from everyone from soldiers in war to figures from history. Our classrooms could be filled with the writing and receiving of letters, notes, cards, memos and, of course, e-mail. All of these are useful sources for poetry writing.
- Searching the Internet and Web sites can provide a rich data bank for locating information. With guidance, the electronic search can open up worlds of knowledge to young researchers. Appropriate software, CD-ROMs, videotapes, and films can give students access to information, often in a dramatic documentary form, that will motivate them to create poems.

Afternoon on a Hill

I will be the gladdest thing
Under the sun!
I will touch a hundred flowers
And not pick one.
I will look at cliffs and clouds
With quiet eyes,
Watch the wind bow down the
    grass,
And the grass rise.
And when lights begin to
    show
Up from the town,
I will mark where must be
    mine,
And then start down!

Edna St. Vincent Millay

- Besides in-person interviews, students can conduct conversations on the phone, by e-mail, or on a chat line on the computer. Poets are not always available for interviews, but printed conversations are sometimes available in journals or in books about writers. It may be just as significant to interview people who experienced the incident described in a poem: a man who spent his life working in a mine may have as much to say as the poet who wrote about mining.
- Students creating poems will have new reasons for using references such as the encyclopedia, all types of dictionaries, the *Guinness Book of World Records*, maps and atlases, telephone directories, and statistics.
- Documents offer special insights for poetry writing: letters and diaries, wills, archival photos, vintage books, land deeds and surveys, reproduced or downloaded from the Internet.
- Fiction may serve as a poetry source.
- Written instructions require writers to organize ideas carefully and these may provide helpful patterns for poems.
- Writing reports, articles, and editorials offers young people opportunities for incorporating both information and their own perspectives and viewpoints into their poem projects.
- Opinion writing, such as advertisements and commercials, reviews, letters, advice columns, speeches, editorials, and debates, can be useful resources for developing poems.

Students who keep notebooks or journals will often find ideas that they can use to create poems. Teachers may encourage them to make these sorts of entries:

- writing about special events at home
- noting unusual pet behaviors
- sketching observations of happenings at school and at home
- gluing in copies of special poems or letters to be used as ideas for their own poems
- describing books and films they have enjoyed
- remembering characters and incidents in books they have read
- writing down memorable quotations
- including photos of families and friends
- retelling family stories as poems
- freezing moments in time
- recording specific ideas for poems
- creating webs of ideas about interesting issues
- getting something off their minds
- working through problems
- naming their worries
- recording their hopes and dreams

A Poetic Documentary

A Demonstration

With the help of their teacher, Angela Rokne; Grades 3–4 students at Calgary's Hawkwood Elementary School marked events in their city's history through responses to photographs taken through the years. They shared their work through a book of poetry they created together. Sample poems by students appear below.

Sandstone Buildings

Standing still
Looking at
Three white cloth covered wagons
Pulled by strong work horses
There on Stephen Avenue's wet dirt road
The settlers in wagons, with sore muscles
Aching bones hoping
To find homes in the
Small new city called Calgary

Shawna

Going Home

I'm traveling along a dirt road
I see the back of a wagon
And beyond
I see the enormous prairies
Smell the fresh cut wood
For our new house
I stick my head out of the wagon
And hear my father's strong voice.

Erin

Crowfoot 1830–1890

A dream maker is born
A peace maker has come
To his people the blackfoot
United the tribes Peigan and Blood
Signed Treaty Seven
Helped his people change
From nomad to farmer
Did he dream
That his name would
Appear on Calgary maps?

Dylan

Buffalo

I gaze into the golden wheat fields watching
The settlers destroy everything I love
Taking away our homes
Forcing us into land we don't want
The iron road slices across our sacred hunting
Ground
Travelers take shots at buffalo leaving them lie.

Giant piles of bones lie by the tracks
We have broken our promises.

Kasim and Brody

- Choose an important event from the history of your community.
- Begin your research to learn all you can about the topic.
- Select a picture, photograph, or document that attracts your interest.
- Create a poem about the image or document to express your thoughts and feelings.

Capturing Historical Moments

On Having Tea with the Famous Five

I sit in Emily's chair
She tells me all her troubles and her dreams
Her open hand waits willingly for someone
To come and sit in her chair as I have
I wonder of Emily's adventure
What does it mean to not be a person
What did Emily feel?
I can see anger in her eyes
I smell the light layer of dust on her bronze
   skirt
I look across the mall at the blowing dust
Still, I sit down to tea with Henrietta and
   Louise
Louise has a warm smile
She begins to tell me about
Voting against liquor and beer
She tells me that some men spend all their
money on beer

While their women and children go without
Henrietta agrees with Louise and says
That's why we drink tea
She offers me a cup of tea
It has the sweet smell of ginger
The touch of her metal hand so smooth and
   tender
I walk over to Nellie and Irene
Nellie holds up the news
   Women are persons
Irene has a twinkle in her eye
This is the most exciting moment in their
   lives
   We are persons
Nelly is happy and proud
They do not feel the cold wind and the
   snow
Blowing against them

Dayna

Dear Diary

Last night I slept on the
Cold, damn muddy ground of
The Canadian Prairies.
In the morning
When the sun rises
We will pack up again
And ride toward the horizon.

We struggle to survive
There are no trees for miles
The few we do see
Seem so close
That we could reach out and touch them
As they shimmer into the green distance

We will never give up as long as the river
   flows

Lindsay and Shannon

Council Meeting

I sit at a council meeting waiting for
MY dad who wants to open a store
   downtown
I am the little boy in the corner
The people look at me
Are they thinking
Who is he?
What is he doing here?
I feel scared with all the
Important people staring at me in my stiff
   new
Clothes
I've never been in such a big room
With its tall skinny windows
And its six oil lamps

Tyler

Playing with Metaphor

The Sea

The sea is a hungry dog,
Giant and grey
He rolls on the beach all day
With his clashing teeth and shaggy jaws
Hour upon hour he gnaws
The rumbling tumbling stones,
And 'Bones, bones, bones, bones!'
The giant sea-dog moans,
Licking his greasy paws

And when the night wind roars
And the moon rocks in the stormy cloud,
He bounds to his feet and snuffs and sniffs
Shaking his wet sides over the cliffs,
And howls and howls long and loud

But on quiet days in May or June
When even the grasses on the dune
Play no more their reedy tune,
With his head between his paws
He lies on the sandy shores,
So quiet, so quiet, he scarcely snores

James Reeves

- "The Sea" is an example of a poem structured as a metaphor. What examples of these types of poems can you collect?
- You can create a metaphor poem by using the name of a famous person. After selecting your name, jot down answers to questions such as these:

What animal does he or she resemble ?
What piece of furniture does he or she resemble?
What food does this person make you think of?
What time of day?

Your answers will form the basis for your poem. The poem below is one example.

He is a bounding leopard;
He is a giant coat tree;
He is a can of Coke Classic;
He is the energy of sunrise;
He is Vince Carter!

Hidden Poetry

Writing that is not poetry can have poetic qualities. When you come across something that makes you think of poetry, you have a "found" poem. Sometimes, you can shape the lines so that they look more like a poem; however, you can't change the words.

- Search cookbooks, restaurant menus, signs in your community, advertisements, and food labels to find examples of words that attract attention and stimulate feelings and memories.
- Use your findings to experiment with arranging the lines or repeating a line or a word. Move words around until you get the shape you want. You can prepare your "found" poem for a presentation.
- In groups, work with the *Joy of Cooking* recipe "Toasted Sandwiches" to make it a "found" poem. Perhaps each group could work with one verse. How many ways can your group find to say the words aloud? Everyone should be hungry when you are all finished.
- Bring in recipes from home that can be treated as "found" poems.

Toasted Sandwiches

Put between 2 slices of toast
any of the following combinations:

sliced chicken
sautéed bacon
shredded cheese
hot sauce or
a cold dressing

creamed chicken
parmesan cheese
grilled tomatoes and bacon

sliced bacon
sliced chicken
mayonnaise
lettuce

Lettuce, French dressing
sliced tomato and avocado
crisp sautéed bacon

Sliced baked ham
Creamed chicken
and mushrooms

Arnold Adoff's Wonderful Shapes

Arnold Adoff was born and raised in the East Bronx section of New York City. In his childhood, "books and food, recipes and political opinions, Jewish poetry and whether the dumplings would float on top of the soup" were all of equal importance. "I read everything in the house," he says, "and then all I could carry home each week from the libraries I could reach on the Bronx buses."

After teaching for 12 years, he turned to writing full time and lectures and conducts workshops across the United States. "Writing a poem is making music with words and space," he says. "A fine poem combines the elements of meaning, music, and a form like a living frame that holds it together."

Sweet.
You are at the line.   You take a deep breath.
        You take a deep breath.
You know: a free throw
        is really
        a free throw:
        no hands in your face;
        no race down
the court;
        no block,
        no clock.

This is the place to score. This is the time to pour it in,
        and beat those nasty bad guys on the other team,
        once and for all.
This is the time to win this game.
You bounce the ball once, and wish for all the luck
        you know you don't need.
You shoot, and the ball
flies
        and arcs and speeds down through
        the hoop to meet the net.
You get your point; your score; your wish.   Swish.
        Sweet

Love Letters, illustrated by Lisa Desimini
OUTside INside Poems, illustrated by John Steptoe
Slow Dance Heart Break Blues, with artwork by William Cotton
Sports Pages, illustrated by Steve Kuzma
Street Music: City Poems, illustrated by Karen Barbour
Today We Are Brother and Sister, illustrated by Glo Coalson

Appendix 1:   The Poetry Unit by Nancy Steele

Poetry and adolescence were made for each other. As young minds begin to question almost everything, poetry provides the perfect place to put those questions into words, to play with ideas, to spill out emotions. And one should not discount the ratio of effort to result. As one of my students commented: "Poems are fun to write. They're fast and less work than stories. A poem can say it all in just a few lines." Who cannot remember and relate to the feelings in "The Note"?

The Note

People know before I do
They're looking at me
Depressed
I unfurl the note
I expected it
Sorrow creeps over and
Around my history book
Sitting in its folds.
I'll deal with it later.

Almost all the writing my students do is related to their lives in meaningful ways. Through their stories, plays, and poems, students have reflected on many of the most important experiences of their lives, both joyful and traumatic. One student spent a year writing about her father's death and her feelings about it. Another child, in Grade 7, wrote about helping her father through family difficulties.

Hold Daddy

Abandoned ... yet together, like orphaned twins
The ripe golden wheat ... the red jacket ... my lunch pail ...
he took it from my hand, and sat
And they were gone, like water running through stones.
Only the man, the girl, and the wind.
He sits and weeps, torrents of grief, like a broken dam
I must comfort, put away my pain.
I must care for him now
I think I was all of seven

I often ask my graduating students if they like writing, if they have a favorite form, if it has helped them, if they would do it without being assigned to do so. Most are confident and proud of the writing they have done. Some recognize that through their writing of poems and scripts, they have come to understandings that they would not have had. A few say they know they will want to write all their lives. Almost all agree that they would never have done any of the work that they are most proud of—the stories, poems, plays, or essays—if they had not been required to do so for assignments. Writing is difficult work.

Generally, poetry is either the second or third writing unit each year. It is heralded by the clearing of all the books of student-written stories from my table. In their place I stack books of student-written poems which, like the storybooks, I have published each year for as long as I have taught writing. On the day we start poetry, I make sure everyone has one or two of the little publications and everyone is asked to look for a poem to share. The poems, like the poets, are, in turn, racy, rude, tender, and funny. They range emotionally from ecstasy to despair. There is something there for everyone.

Sometimes, I hear the Grade 7s grumble about how the poems are too good. They could never write poems like these. I am careful to explain that every student has at least two poems in each book each year, so yes, somehow everyone does write two wonderful poems. But these poems are *not* first drafts, nor do they come out of nowhere. I will give them specific instructions that will help them find the words they want. Some begin to relax. Most don't.

By our second poetry class most people have written something. The poets can be coaxed to share, especially after the braver ones have been well received. I ask if they want to read the poem themselves or have me read it. They often ask me to read for them, probably because it is fun to hear their words from another's mouth. As with our story conferences, the first responses are about what we liked about the poem. I sometimes start by pointing out the fresh use of a word or a lively image. The class joins in, usually saying, "It was really good," but eventually making more specific comments. Finally, at the poet's request, the class makes suggestions for changes that might lead to greater clarity or less repetition. The poet takes notes and next class, if there is time, will read a second draft. There is never enough time to give all the poems the attention they deserve ...

At the end of the unit each student must submit ten poems. I introduce about ten different ideas on ways to write poems (haiku, acrostics, concrete poems, cinquains, extended comparisons, even limericks, though I generally eschew rhyme). I ask that they choose eight forms and write a poem using each. Their last two poems may be their own choice or free verse. As I introduce each idea, I read poems written by previous students or by published poets that use that idea or form. We talk about metaphor, simile, and personification. We read poems noting the poet's use of assonance or alliteration. We talk about the use of line breaks to extend meaning. I try to bring in poets to talk about their own work. When the unit is drawing to a close, we have a class to which the students each bring the ten poems they have written. Every poet puts a star next to the two he or she likes the best. Then the packages of poems are passed about the class to be read. People put their initials next to their two favorites. The poems are returned to the poets and eventually to me. Often, but not always, I agree with the majority vote.

Appendix 2: Poetry Events by Larry Swartz

Some Poems by the Students in Room 203

A bird without wings,
A world without sky
A clock without hands,
Is like a reason without why.

A picture without paint,
A group without a leader,
A song without notes,
Is like a book without a reader.

Matt

Books are like barbecued
    steaks—
        Sometimes tender
        Sometimes juicy
        Sometimes well done.
How do you like yours?
Me?
        I like mine with
            lots of spice
            lots of flavour
            lots of meat
            lots to savour.

Liza

The trees look up at the sky
The sky looks down at the
    water
The water looks up at the
    clouds
And the clouds look down at
    me.

Chris

My program, I felt, was rich with picture books and novels, but I recognized the need to pay attention to poems and one summer, in the middle of my career, two things influenced my understanding of teaching through poetry: I attended a conference and heard Georgia Heard speak about teaching poetry and was inspired by her passion and the ideas she offered for creating poems on life experiences. Also, I carefully read *Poems Please!* by David Booth and Bill Moore. When I went back to my classroom in September, I challenged myself to enrich my language program by spending more time with poetry and to help the students in my Grade 4/5 class to recognize the value of poetry as an art experience. I hoped to enhance the children's learning not only for reading and writing, but also for chanting, singing, discussing, arguing, responding, interpreting, questioning, performing, role playing, painting, and dancing.

Throughout the year I organized events that allowed my students to explore and experience the scope of poetry in all its forms. By year's end the class had met more than 300 poems written by professional poets, by their peers, and by their teacher. Students read poems by themselves, in small groups, and as a whole class. They read poems quietly and aloud. They talked with others about the poems they read or wrote responses to poems in their reading journals. They wrote poems short and long. They wrote poems stimulated by a theme or topic, prompted by the poetry of others, or patterned on a poetic form. Occasionally, they revised their poems and prepared published forms of their work to be shared with others.

I recognize that students sometimes need shape and pattern to assist them in their struggle to write poems. When they examine the way that words are placed on paper by poets (as well as by their friends), they might be encouraged to create original poems using patterns that they find engaging. Form can give students a sense of control and economy as they write. Having said this, I have some hesitation about teaching the writing of poetry in this fashion. When students write formula poems, which are usually short and written to specific criteria, they might see poetry as a paint-by-number exercise where they fill in spaces according to rules. Sometimes, I have offered suggestions to comply with poetic patterns and structures. The students have particularly enjoyed writing concrete shape poems, poems with a repeated line pattern, list poems, and poems of 20 words or less. At other times, I have woven poetry events into themes or curriculum topics experienced throughout the year. The students have written poems to accompany paintings by the Group of Seven and their own artwork, to express their feelings about reading, and to reflect on world events. They have written poems on the computer, in their notebooks, on the bulletin board, on small file cards, on the blackboard, on chart paper, and on overhead transparencies. Some poems remained in their notebooks, some were developed into published pieces, and some were chosen to be part of an anthology produced each term to share with others in the school and with their families.

Golden trees
Stand around me.

Green hills
Sleep beside me.

Swan-like clouds
Fly above me

And my soul rings
Like a church bell.

Trevor

Beetles for breakfast
Spiders for lunch
Lizards for dinner
Munch!
Munch!
Munch!

Connie

The Pet Store

10 guinea pigs wobbling
9 snakes slithering.
8 parrots squawking.
7 mice munching.
6 gerbils scurrying.
5 puppies yapping.
4 fish wiggling.
3 monkeys laughing.
2 kittens leaping.
1 hamster sleeping.

Josh

40 Poetry Events
1. Poem of the day: read by the teacher
2. Poem of the day: read by students who have rehearsed the reading
3. Choose a favorite poem of the week or month.
4. Celebrate the work of a poet.
5. Explore whole-class shared reading of favorite poems.
6. Have students read poems aloud chorally in small groups.
7. Prepare a presentation of a long poem by assigning different parts to individuals and groups.
8. Prepare snippets of poetry to be displayed around the classroom or the school.
9. Write poems as graffiti on a bulletin board display.
10. Write a personal definition of poetry.
11. Develop a class book with each student creating a page illustrating a line or part of a poem.
12. Write a response to a poem.
13. Brainstorm a list of questions about a poem.
14. Organize discussion in pairs, small groups, or the whole class.
15. Build a class anthology of favorite published poems.
16. Assemble a class anthology of student-authored poems.
17. Make a tape recording of favorite poems.
18. Use a poem as a stimulus for illustration.
19. Rearrange lines of a poem that have been mixed up.
20. Sing a poem.
21. Transcribe familiar rhymes that are ringing inside the head.
22. Find new poems in the library.
23. Read poems together with a buddy.
24. Transform a passage from a novel into a free verse poem.
25. Find poetry in the newspaper, on billboards, on labels, in recipes, in dictionaries, in instructions, and so on.
26. Collect appealing, strange, or unfamiliar words found in poems.
27. Create displays of poetry anthologies. Change them frequently.
28. Share poems from a variety of cultures.
29. Read a picture book told in narrative verse (e.g., *Hooray for Diffendorfer Day!* by Dr. Seuss)
30. Use poems as a source for dance drama or movement.
31. Ask the students: What makes a poem good?
32. Invent a story about a nursery rhyme.
33. Invite the students to role-play and interview characters from a poem.
34. Borrow a title, first line, rhyme scheme, or form of a poem to create a new poem.
35. Offer alternative titles to poems.
36. Compare two poems.
37. Compare two poets.
38. Write at least one poem for the children.
39. Organize a Poetry Club during the noon hour or after school.
40. Let the poem be.

Appendix 3: Teaching Poetry from the Heart by Eddie Ing

What is beauty?
the great blue sea
the mountains as high as the
  sky
the animals roaming free
the forest filled with trees
the bottom of the ocean
the snow on the mountains
the animal's footprint
the raindrops
the world in which I live
That is beauty!

Jaclyn

Blue
Likes nuts
Urban Habitat
Eggs
Juniper Tree
Always hungry
Young have no feathers

Nest
Eats insects
Seeds are favourite food
Tree Dweller

Julian

Jelly Fish

Jelly Fish sparkle
In the dark depths of the sea
I swim among them

Journey

Poetry matters in my classroom. I have learned that feelings can be unusual things and that they are not always convenient. I have also learned that emotions are at the heart of my creativity. Creativity is unusual stuff. It frightens. It is subversive. It mistrusts what it sees, what it hears. It dares to doubt. It acts even if it errs. It infiltrates preconceived notions. It rattles established certitudes. It incessantly invents new ways to communicate, new vocabularies. It provokes and changes points of view.

When one writes poetry, packed with emotions, feelings, sensations, and opinions, the important thing is that it is good for the soul. Writing poetry is a process that develops over time. It can reflect our emotional growth.

I read the children in my class a poem a day for the first month of school. Many favorites include poems by Shel Silverstein, Jack Prelutsky, Eloise Greenfield, and my own poems. I photocopy the poem and project it on the overhead so that the children can read along. I purposely leave out the traditional grammar of commas and periods, the capitals. Doing this allows them to see the raw piece of literature without the clutter.

I discuss with them the shape of the poem—the rhyme or the rhythm—in a very informal way. I ask their opinions of what the author is saying. I scaffold ways for them to interact with a piece of literature, repeating daily these ways of learning and knowing. After the first month, children sign up on a monthly schedule, identifying what they would like to read to the class. All students are expected to present a piece of literature. It can be their own poem or a short passage. Some discussions have taken up the entire morning, rich with inquiry and cooperative learning.

It is important to expose students to many forms of creativity, to try to link their emotions with these forms, perhaps inspiring them to write in free verse. However, we also need to provide explicit instruction in reading and writing, so that they can all acquire the strategies that will help them to read and write more complex and meaningful texts.

It is important for me to support my students in their reading and writing in a variety of genres and text structures found across the curriculum. To do this I use books that children have discovered, traditional spellers and grammar books to find the "meat and potatoes" of instruction and then introduce these structures in the form of poetry under a blanket of different forms and styles. We have studied many forms of expression in poetry, including acrostic, alliteration, alphabet, catalogue, cento, cinquain, clerihew, couplet, definition, diamante, free verse, haiku, hyperbole, limerick, lyric, metaphor/simile, and onomatopoeia. Each form was introduced by a whole-class discussion. To take away the anxiety, I would model writing several poems in front of the class, accepting suggestions from my students. Within 15 minutes there were poems produced by "us" in the form we were studying that day. Children were then asked to produce a poem in rough draft by themselves, and discussions and their resultant ideas were encouraged throughout the work period.

To conclude each form, the children's writing went through a draft phase, an editing phase, and a good copy phase. Each student had the opportunity to choose their own decorative piece of writing paper from the stock I had bought.

100

The Falling Star

Looking at the stars
Makes me feel so sleepy
But sooner than later
The moon surrenders itself
To look at me
Its gleaming face
Stares down at me
While I stare back at it
It seems like a
Sort
Of
Sign
That
Hope
Is
To
Come with the falling star
That I must catch

Ellen

Between our free verse writing and our formal instructional writing, children were able to complete at least one piece of writing per month which we celebrated as a class in book form. Each member voted for the titles of our books, with the most popular title placed on the cover of each book.

Poems convey strong feelings. One gets a little thump in one's heart when they are read, partly because poems aren't afraid to tell the truth. Poetry can be utterly honest. Some students find it natural to be honest in their poetry; for others it is much more difficult. Sometimes, it is difficult to be honest with yourself.

I teach today the way my family taught me—from the heart.

Appendix 4: Building a Classroom Poetry Program

❑ Do you read poems aloud to the students on a regular basis?

❑ Are you developing your own skills of presenting poetry out loud effectively?

❑ Do you invite guest readers from different countries and cultures, and with different dialects, to come to your classroom *or* make available audio and visual recordings of poems?

❑ Do you integrate poetry into different curriculum areas, as well as making a special time for poetry?

❑ Do you have a classroom collection of poetry books for student use, including during independent reading?

❑ Do you involve the school library and the public library in your poetry exploration?

❑ Do you use the Internet sites for student poetry activities, including the Web sites of different poets?

❑ Do students experience different types of anthologies, from single poet collections to themed anthologies?

❑ Do the students read poetry aloud in a variety of groupings (solo to whole class)?

❑ How do you encourage the memorization of favorite poems?

❑ Do your students write poetry from a variety of stimuli (their reading, personal experiences, special events, and curriculum topics)?

❑ Are students sharing the poems they write, both in print and aloud?

❑ Do you encourage wordplay with vocabulary, sounds, patterns, games, ads, rhymes, and so on?

❑ Do you maximize student discussion of poetry through small groups, literature circles, and seminars?

❑ What strategies do you employ for revisiting poems and mining them for depth of ideas?

❑ Do you expose the class to a variety of genres, styles, and formats of poetry?

❑ Do you explore different poetic structures and forms (e.g., not all poems have to rhyme)?

❑ Are students gaining knowledge about how poems work from "experiencing" as opposed to "being told"?

❑ Are you introducing the students to poets from a variety of districts, backgrounds, countries, and cultures who demonstrate the many styles that poetry embraces?

❑ Do you teach poetry as a text to be interpreted and considered as opposed to poems used as "fillers" in a reading text?

❑ Are the students connecting poetry to the other arts—singing, drama, photography, computers, illustration, dance?

❑ Are you making connections to the poetic world of pop culture through hip-hop, rap, rock, reggae, and more?

❑ Are you using a variety of presentational forms for poetry—books, overhead transparencies, computers, charts, mobiles, and tapes?

❑ Are the children storying with the poems they read, that is, telling and retelling stories found between the lines, exploring both text and subtext, inferring, predicting, and questioning as they build narratives?

❑ Are the students creating their own anthologies, learning to select and arrange poems and poets?

❑ Are the students exploring Web sites of poets and poems?

❑ Do students share poems with one another, with other classes, with parents, with other schools, and with other Web sites?

Appendix 5: The Poetry Shelf

On the lists below, we have identified many of our favorite poets. These are the artists we turn to in building resources for our poetry programs for young people. In this book, you will find most information on the poets whose names are italicized; one-page features appear at the end of each chapter.

Since some of a poet's books may be difficult to find, we suggest that you begin with any available books by a poet you enjoy, as well as visiting Web sites by and about poets. We celebrate the poets and anthologists who have enriched our work and our lives.

1: The Patterns in Poems
Jack Prelutsky
Eleanor Farjeon
John Mole
Shel Silverstein
Kristine O'Connell George
John Foster
Karla Kuskin
Lois Lenski
Bill Martin Jr.
James Reeves
Mary Ann Hoberman

2: Poetry as Wordplay
Diane Dawber
Richard Edwards
Robert Heidbreder
Carolyn Graham
Kali Dakos
X. J. Kennedy
Roger McGough
Jeff Moss
Judith Viorst
Mary O'Neill
R. L. Stevenson
Sheree Fitch

3: Mother Goose's Family
Dennis Lee
Sonja Dunn
Robert Priest
Loris Lesynski
Arnold Lobel
Iona and Peter Opie

Edward Lear
Eve Merriam
Wendy and Clyde Watson

4: Painting Images with Words
James Berry
David Bouchard
Ted Hughes
Valerie Bloom
Maya Angelou
Donald Hall
Dionne Brand
Ralph Fletcher
Cynthia Rylant
Nikki Giovanni

5: Hearing Voices
Michael Rosen
Judith Nicholls
Jon Agard
Grace Nichols
Eloise Greenfield
Vachel Lindsay
Kit Wright
Seamus Heaney
Nikki Grimes
Paul Fleischman

6: Uncovering the Stories
Naomi Shihab Nye
Walter de la Mare
Brian Patten
Robert Frost
Langston Hughes
Ian Seraillier
Jean Little
Charles Causley

7: Exploring Games and Ceremonies
Joseph Bruchac
Jane Yolen
Richard Lewis
Janet and Allan Ahlberg
Byrd Baylor
Gary Soto

8: Responding Through Poetry

Arnold Adoff

Gerard Benson

Douglas Florian

James Stevenson

Lee Bennett Hopkins

Carl Sandburg

Paul Janeczko

Janet S. Wong

Valerie Worth

Myra Cohn Livingston

Gareth Owen

Professional Reading

Barrs, Myra Ellis Sue. 1996. *Hands on Poetry: Using Poetry in the Classroom*. London: CLPE.

Booth, David, and Bill Moore. 2003. *Poems Please! Sharing Poetry with Children*. Markham, ON: Pembroke.

Cecil, Nancy Lee. 1997. *For the Love of Poetry: Literacy Scaffolds, Extension Ideas, and More*. Winnipeg, MB: Peguis.

Chatfield, Heather, and Shirley Lacey. 1989. *Let's Enjoy Poetry: A Poetry Program for Primary Children*. Melbourne, Australia: Longman Cheshire.

Copeland, Jeffrey S. 1993. *Speaking of Poets: Interviews with Poets Who Write for Children and Young Adults*. Urbana, IL: National Council of Teachers of English.

Cullinan, Bernice E., Marilyn C. Scala, and Virginia C. Schroder. 1995. *Three Voices: An Invitation to Poetry Across the Curriculum*. Portland, ME: Stenhouse/Markham, ON: Pembroke.

Esbensen, Barbara Juster. 1995. *A Celebration of Bees: Helping Children Write Poetry*. New York: Henry Holt and Company.

Fletcher, Ralph. 2002. *Poetry Matters: Writing a Poem from the Inside Out*. New York: HarperTrophy.

Flynn, Nick, and Shirley McPhillips. 2000. *A Note Slipped Under the Door: Teaching from Poems We Love*. Portland, ME: Stenhouse.

Fox, John. 1995. *Finding What You Didn't Lose: Expressing Your Truth and Creativity Through Poem-Making*. New York: A Jeremy P. Tarcher.

Glover, Mary Kenner. 1999. *A Garden of Poets: Poetry Writing in the Elementary Classroom*. Urbana, IL: National Council of Teachers of English.

Graves, Donald H. 1992. *Explore Poetry*. Portsmouth, NH: Heinemann.

Heard, Georgia. 1995. *Writing Toward Home: Tales ancd Lessons to Find Your Way*. Portsmouth, NH: Heinemann.

_____. 1999. *Awakening the Heart: Exploring Poetry in Elementary and Middle School*. Portsmouth, NH: Heinemann.

Hughes, Ted. 1967. *Poetry in the Making*. London: Faber and Faber.

Ioannou, Susan. 2000. *A Magical Clockwork: The Art of Writing the Poem*. Toronto: Wordwrights Canada.

Janeczko, Paul. 1999. *How to Write Poetry*. New York: Scholastic.

_____., comp. 2002. *Seeing the Blue Between: Advice and Inspiration for Young Poets*. Cambridge, MA: Candlewick Press.

Koch, Kenneth. 1974. *Rose, Where Did You Get That Red?: Teaching Great Poetry to Children*. New York: Vintage Books.

Koch, Kenneth, and Kate Farrell. 1982. *Sleeping on the Wing: An Anthology of Modern Poetry with Essays on Reading and Writing*. New York: Vintage Books.

Larrick, Nancy. 1991. *Let's Do a Poem: Introducing Poetry to Children Through Listening, Singing, Chanting, Impromptu Choral Reading, Body Movement, Dance, and Dramatization*. New York: Delacorte Press.

Livingston, Myra Cohn. 1991. *Poem-making: Ways to Begin Writing Poetry*. New York: A Charlotte Zolotow Book.

_____, ed. 1997. *I Am Writing a Poem About a Game of Poetry*. New York: Margaret K. McElderry Books.

Moyers, Bill. 1995. *The Language of Life: A Festival of Poets*. New York: Broadway Books.

Padgett, Ron, ed. 1987. *The Teachers & Writers Handbook of Poetic Forms*. New York: Teachers & Writers Collaborative.

Parsons, Les. 1992. *Poetry, Themes, and Activities: Exploring the Fun and Fantasy of Language*. Markham, ON: Pembroke.

Peck, Richard. 2002. *Invitations to the World: Teaching and Writing for the Young*. New York: Dial Books.

Swartz, Larry. 1993. *Classroom Events Through Poetry*. Markham, ON: Pembroke.

Sweeney, Jacqueline. 1993. *Teaching Poetry: Yes You Can!* New York: Scholastic.

Tiedt, Iris McClellan. 2002. *Tiger Lilies, Toadstools, and Thunderbolts: Engaging K-8 Students with Poetry*. Newark, DE: International Reading Association.

Tsujimoto, Joseph I. 1988. *Teaching Poetry Writing to Adolescents*. Urbana, IL: National Council of Teachers of English.

Acknowledgments

Every effort has been made to contact and acknowledge all sources of material in this book. The publishers would be grateful if any errors or omissions were pointed out, so that they may be corrected.

"Longhouse Song" by Joseph Bruchac, in Janeczko, P. 2002. *Seeing the Blue Between: Advice and Inspirations for Young Poets,* Cambridge, MA: Candlewick Press.

"The Question" by Dennis Lee, in Lee, D. and Newfeld, F. 1963. *Nicholas Knock and Other People: Poems*, Toronto: Macmillan of Canada.

"If You Could Wear My Sneakers" by Sheree Fitch, in Fitch, S. 1997. *If You Could Wear My Sneakers!*, Toronto: Doubleday.

"CAT Began" by Andrew Matthews, in Greenaway, Theresa. 1995. *Paws and Claws*, London: Hutchinson Children's Books.

"Bingo" by Paul Janeczko, in Janeczko, P. 1990. *The Place My Words Are Looking For*, New York: Bradbury Press (an affiliate of MacMillan, Inc.).

"Grandpa" by Berlie Doherty, in Doherty, B. 1999. *Walking on Air*, London: Hodder Children's Books.

"What Is Under" by Tony Mitton, in Mitton, T. 1998. *Plum*, London: Scholastic Children's Books.

"The Fruit Seller" by Peter Jailall, in Jailall, P. 2003. *When September Comes*, Toronto: Natural Heritage Books.

"Sea Timeless Song" by Grace Nichols, in Nichols, G. 1988. *Come on into My Tropical Garden: Poems for Children.* London: Black; Philadelphia: Lippincott.

"Down Behind the Dustbin" by Michael Rosen, in Rosen, M. 1981. *You Can't Catch Me*, NY & London: Andre Deutsch.

"Biking" by Judith Nicholls, in Nicholls, J. 1987. *Midnight Forest and Other Poems*, London: Faber and Faber Ltd.

"Natasha Green" by Ian McMillan, in McMillan, I. 1998. *I Found This Shirt: Poems and Prose from the Centre*, Manchester, UK: Carcanet Press.

"One for the Man" by Charles Causley, in Causley, C. 1986. *Early in the Morning*, London: Puffin Books.

"Knocking the Wind Out" by Diane Dawber, in Dawber, D. 1997. *How Do You Wrestle a Goldfish?*, Nepean, ON: Borealis Press.

"Looking for Snow Fleas" by Diane Dawber (unpublished).

"Pumpkin, Pumpkin" by John Agard, in Agard, J. 1991. *No Hickory, No Dickory, No Dock*, London: Puffin Books.

"Old Man Ocean" by Russell Hoban, in Hoban, R. 1990. *The Pedalling Man*, London: William Heinemann Limited.

"Names and Nicknames" by James Reaney, in Reaney, J. 1990. *Performance Poems*, Goderich, ON: Moonstone Press.

"Clear the Fluff!" by Michael Rosen, in Rosen, M. 1981. *You Can't Catch Me*, NY & London: Andre Deutsch.

"My Hard Repair Job" by James Berry, in Berry, J. 1988. *When I Dance*, London: Hamish Hamilton.

"The Titanic" by Gillian Clark, in Clark, C. 1999. *The Animal Wall*, Wales, UK: Pont Books, Gomer Press.

"The Multilingual Mynah Bird" by Jack Prelutsky, from *Zoo Doings* in Prelutsky, J. 1997. *The Beauty of the Beast*, New York: Knopf.

"Welcome to Abu Dhabi" by Naomi Shihab Nye, in Nye, N. S. 2002. *The Flag of Childhood: Poems from the Middle East*, New York: Aladdin Paperbacks.

"The Muddy Puddle" by Dennis Lee, in Lee, D. 1983. *Jelly Belly*, Toronto: Macmillan of Canada.

"Hurricane" by James Berry. 1988. Peters Fraser & Dunlop Group Limited.

"The Grasshopper and the Ants" by Jane Yolen, in Yolen, J. 1995. *A Sip of Aesop*, New York: Blue Sky Press.

"Sweet" by Arnold Adolf, in Adolf, A. 1986. *Sport Pages*, New York: HarperCollins.

"Remembering Basketball Daze" by Charles R. Smith, in Smith, C. R. 1999. *Rimshots: Basketball Picks, Rolls, and Rhythms*, New York: Dutton Children's Books.

"How Computers Can Enhance Poetry Writing" from the journal *Language Matters* published by the Centre for Literacy in Primary Education.

"Four a.m. in the Woods" by Marilyn Nelson, in Nelson, M. 2001. *Carver: A Life in Poems*, Asheville, NC: Front Street Books.

"The Dragons Are Singing Tonight" by Jack Prelutsky, in Prelutsky, J. 1993. *The Dragons Are Singing Tonight*, New York: Scholastic Inc.

Index